Elbridge Gerry's Letterbook

*It is the duty of every man though he
may have but one day to live to devote
that day to the good of his country.*

ELBRIDGE GERRY

ELBRIDGE GERRY'S LETTERBOOK

Paris 1797 – 1798

Edited by
RUSSELL W. KNIGHT

SALEM, MASSACHUSETTS

THE ESSEX INSTITUTE

1966

Printed in the U.S.A. by The Anthoensen Press, Portland, Maine

Introduction

SEVERAL years ago it was my good fortune to acquire the Letter-book kept by Elbridge Gerry while he was in Paris, France, and deeply involved in what is now labeled the XYZ Affair. Gerry and his fellow ministers, Charles Cotesworth Pinckney and John Marshall, did their utmost to resolve the crisis that had ruptured Franco-American relations. However, when it ultimately became clear that an amicable settlement with the Directoire appeared impossible, unless accompanied by a bribe, they decided to abandon negotiations and return to the United States.

For the part they played in the unsuccessful discussions, two of the commissioners won a measure of fame: the efforts of the third member went for nought. In truth, all Elbridge Gerry received in the way of a reward for his role in this melodramatic episode was censure, condemnation, indignities and unmerited abuse.

It is my hope that the publication of his Paris Letterbook will invalidate much of the obloquy that has been heaped upon Gerry's head. Since the contents of the correspondence compressed between its covers were personal and private, the feisty little emissary often expressed his opinions rather freely to his wife. As a result, his shrewd and frequently pungent observations will unquestionably provide historians and scholars with new and significant insights in respect to Gerry's part in the XYZ negotiations.

Although every effort has been made to identify the persons and places mentioned in the Letterbook, there are a few exceptions. In some instances the individuals require no identification because of their prominence in world affairs, while others are too obscure to trace, or are referred to only casually. I have also deemed it wise to retain the spelling and punctuation used by the author as he penned these letters. While the text might have been improved by some editing, these changes could have altered the thought Gerry was endeavoring to convey and thus innocently caused irreparable harm to the material.

In the course of preparing these letters for publication I frequently encountered some rather exasperating stumbling blocks. That I eventually surmounted them is due in a large measure to the advice and assistance I received from Lyman H. Butterfield, Editor in Chief, The Adams Papers; Julian P. Boyd, Editor, Papers of Thomas Jefferson; Fred W. Shipton, Librarian, U. S. Department of State; and Howard C. Rice, Jr., Chief of Special Collections, Princeton University Library.

I am also indebted to Dr. Henry R. Viets, Curator, Boston Medical Library; to Paul O. Blanchette, Librarian, Peabody Museum of Salem; and to Miss Margaret Hackett, Boston Athenæum, for their expert assistance.

In particular, I owe a debt of gratitude for counsel and encouragement to George Athan Billias, Professor of History, Clark University, who has in preparation the first modern scholarly biography of Gerry; and to Norman R. Bennett, Assistant Professor of History, Boston University, for his many helpful suggestions.

I likewise owe my secretary, Mrs. Sophie Chiluk Deacy, my sincere thanks. She not only typed the entire manuscript, but with an admirable display of persistence and patience deciphered many a baffling phrase.

RUSSELL W. KNIGHT

Marblehead, Massachusetts

The Letters

TO MR. CHARLES C. PINCKNEY[1]

Wednesday Morning

Rotterdam 20th September 1797

My Dear Sir

On Monday noon I arrived in the Ship Union at Hellevoetsluys [a seaport town, 17 miles from Rotterdam] and soon after arrived your friendly letter of the Seventh; your early and particular attention to procure & send to Mrs Gerry the Baume de Fioraventi[2] will produce on her part as it does on mine, a grateful Acknowledgement: & thank you likewise for taking apartments for me at Paris, Where I will endeavor to be in time to meet yourself & General [John] Marshall.[3]

I have hitherto been unfortunate in this enterprise. the Ship was by bad weather detained till the 9th of August & the second day after she sailed I was taken down with a slow putrid Fever from which I did not recover till the Expiration of three weeks. during the first ten days after we left Boston, excepting a Gale of Wind of short duration, the Weather was very pleasant; & in the thirty Subsequent days, we had no less than eighteen of them with Gales of Wind. Being anxious to join you & General Marshall & finding that the progress of the Ship to Rotterdam would be slow, She being at noon yesterday but eight miles from Hellevoetsluys I took passage in A Boat Which landed me about 12 miles from the city. I came from thence in a Close Carriage. But we Arrived in the Evening & I had to cross the river & walk in the rain to the Marshall Tureene Tavern: a risque Which I had no idea of taking after having been confined to the Cabin Almost the Whole Voyage. I hope however it will not produce a relapse. here I find to my mortification, that you left this city yesterday. In consequence of which I think it not probable that I shall have the pleasure of seeing you before my arrival at Paris. I propose to take Brusells & Valenciennes in my rout: after my return from the Hague; to which I shall go this afternoon. it will give Mrs Gerry great pleasure to hear from Mrs

[7]

Pinckney & yourself as she will on receiving a letter which I have just written her. Pray give her my best respects to her, accept them yourself, & present them to General Marshall.

I cannot be sure that it will not be necessary or at least expected for me to see Messrs Willink & Co[4] in which case I shall not remain at Amsterdam more than a day.

NOTES

1. Charles Cotesworth Pinckney (1746-1825), American lawyer, statesman and diplomat, born in Charleston, South Carolina. He was long given credit for having coined the ringing declaration of "millions for defense but not one cent for tribute." Now, however, this phrase is attributed to Robert Goodloe Harper who is said to have voiced it at a testimonial dinner held at Oeler's Hotel, Philadelphia, 18 June 1798. Later, when asked why he had never acknowledged this fact, Pinckney explained, "The nation adopted the expression, and I always thought there would have been more ostentation denying than in submitting the report." Douglas Southall Freeman, *George Washington* (New York, 1949), VII, 515.

2. An aromatic preparation used to soothe, comfort and heal. Mrs. Gerry, suffering from "weak" eyes, received a constant supply of this balm from Europe. Effective or not she continued to use it as long as her husband lived. Fifteen years after the receipt of this letter, and six months before he died in 1814, he was still recommending that she either apply the "Baume" or rose brandy to her eyes for relief.

3. John Marshall (1755-1835), American jurist and Revolutionary soldier who with Gerry and Pinckney composed the American mission to France.

4. Dutch banking house. The United States often obtained loans from this and other financial institutions established in the Netherlands.

TO MR. BOSSENGER FOSTER, JUNIOR[1]

Rotterdam 25th Septr 1797

Mr Bossenger Foster Jr
Dear Sir

Mr Craigie[2] having expressed a wish, that I would appoint you a secretary of my mission to the french republic & it being a proposition perfectly agreeable to my mind, I have refused a number of applicants & reserved the office for yourself. but since my arrival, doubts

[8]

have been suggested to me respecting the effects on the minds of the Directoire, of your long residence in London; & it is indespensibly necessary for me, to ascertain as far as possible this point, to avoid suspicion & embarassment which may otherwise ensue. I shall therefore postpone my final determination, untill my arrival at paris; or untill I can confer with my collegues, should I be able to overtake them on the road. in the interim, I wish you would prepare for the engagement, if you like it: & be ready to come to paris on the shortest notice. perhaps it will be elegible for you to take passage to Havre, & there wait, till you can hear from me: because I am in want of your assistance now, & shall want it more, on my arrival at paris. in that case, if I find it necessary to dispense with your services, which will be very mortifying to me, after the inconveniences resulting from the delay of appointing a secretary, I will endeavor to obtain a passport for you to come to Paris, or to return to London, as may best suit your engagements: & it will be elegible not to communicate ye object of your coming to Havre—I am in want of the books mentioned below, & if the editions are good & the books not injured, second hand books will be as good as new on this occasion. Mr Bayard can inform you on this point, whether the editions are good.—

Galliana[3]		on the	The government constitutions
Puffendorf[4]	}	laws	
Grotius[5]		of nations	The history of the Netherlands

N.B. I want all the books in english & none larger than octavos—if there is no translation of Galliani, you will purchase the french edition—Should you choose not to embark for Havre untill you hear from me, you can send the books in a box to our consul there & inform me of the cost of them & of the Baume for Mrs Gerry.

25th   the letter to Mr Beldemaker[6], Antwerp.
27 Sept Sent a duplicate to Mr Beldeemaker,
         our Consul at Rotterdam—to be
         forwarded to London.

1. Hired by Gerry as his secretary, Bossenger Foster, Jr., assumed his new duties in October. But five months later, in a letter dated 30 March 1798, he submitted his resignation. "It has been" he wrote, "a source of much uneasiness and regret to me that I have been under the necessity of declaring before my inability to get through so much voluminous writing, as has appeared in the course of the negotiations." James T. Austin, *Life of Elbridge Gerry* (Boston, 1829), II, 286.

2. Andrew Craigie (1743-1819), Cambridge, Mass., financier and speculator.

3. Abbé Ferdinand Galiani (1728-1787). Italian writer, economist and philosopher and author of *Della moneta* and *Diologues sur le commerce des blés*.

4. Samuel Pufendorf (1632-1694), German jurist. His published works include the *Elementa jurisprudentia universalis* and *De jure naturae et gentium*.

5. Hugo Grotius (1583-1645), eminent jurist and statesman and author of *De jure belli ae pacis*.

6. John Beeldemaker, presumed to be a citizen of Holland, was appointed United States Consul at Rotterdam 26 June 1797 and held that office until 18 April 1800.

TO CHARLES COTESWORTH PINCKNEY

Brussells 29th Sept 1797

Sent
Major General Pinckney
My Dear Sir

I have received triplicates of your letter of the 22nd & your letter of the 24th was delivered to me here last evening. N.B. not having time to copy ye letter, the following are the heads of ye contents—that had he & not General Marshall not obeyed the call of leaving Rotterdam as they did, it would have given me pain—the circumstances of my voyage & landing at Rotterdam, & acknowledgement of his kindness in procuring the baume were then mentioned, & information was given soon of my making the communication in a letter of ye 19th left with Mr Beldemaker. that I left Rotterdam on ye 19th after dinner, arrived at ye Hague that evening: left it on ye 20th for Amsterdam arrived here that evening—left it at 12 on the 21st arrived at the Hague about ten that evening—waited on ye french minister at ye time he appointed on ye 22nd in ye evening—left the Hague on ye morning of ye 23d dined at Rotterdam—made my arrangements ye next day for Moerdyke [Moerdijk], was detained by ye tide till 6 in ye morning, then sailed & arrived at ye place last mentioned at 6 in ye morning—took a coach from thence for Antwerp, which was exchanged after proceeding one third of ye way for an execrable cabriole with two horses. Should have defended it, if I had carried arms. arrived at Antwerp at 3 in ye evening & made arrangements for hiring a carrᵃ [carriage] to Paris. failing this I bot a post Chair & had it fixed ye next day: & ye day after arrived here. was quite unwell last night: ye fatigue of traveling in wet weather, & by night, & setting up late to make arrangements for ye next day being too great. have communicated his & Mrs P kind remembrance to Mrs G. which will give her great Pleasure. accept his kind offer to make some disposition respecting my household, requesting they may be subject to alterations if necessary. have only my valet, Secretary being in London (this to be confidential) Present my respects to Mrs P[inckney] & G[eneral] Marshall & myself to Miss P[inckney] & ye young gentlemen.

TO MRS GERRY

Mrs Gerry by Capt [Ebenezer] Nutting   Paris 9 Octr 1797
who sailed about 2 or 3ᵈ Novr

I have arrived here my dear Life, the 4ᵗʰ in the evening, & was very kindly received by my Colleagues & Mrs Pinckney, in whose society I promise myself much happiness. I have given you in several letters a history of my adventure to Rotterdam, which was peculiarly unfortunate in circumstances but fortunate in the event. my feelings were for three weeks much affected by pricking my finger with my stock buckel, the day before I embarked. for a long Time I applyed turpentine & this cured it—they were also affected considerably by turning my lame ancle, as I came down from the Consul to take my leave of you. this continued thro passage; in so great a degree as that I was obliged to use the greatest precaution to prevent an increase of the injury. I could not walk in the best weather we had for a month be-

[11]

fore our arrival, across the cabin, with two ropes stretched from the sides to keep me steady, without hurting my ancle. but it is now well & I can use boots—my sickness was serious; I knew it to be dangerous when first attacked, but determined to take the chance of being my own physician, rather than to return. I had a good medical author, Tissot,[1] & followed precisely his directions: & I had a supply as well of medicine, as of other necessaries, which you insisted on putting with my seastores, or I would never have recovered. tamerinds you will recollect you proposed & I really prohibited them: but I would have given for some, their weight in gold. when I wrote from New-foundland I was rather better; but the putrid complaints in conse-quence of my living ten days on acid drinks only were followed with such a sour stomack as not to admit of my taking any thing without its turning instantly acid; I opposed to this alkaline food such as Chicken broth & crackers boiled in it, and found a remedy. at the end of three weeks my appetite returned, & amidst storms and tempests, for we had no good weather after the first ten days. I never enjoyed myself better: being always careful to have the dead light in, to pre-vent the cabin from being wet, which would have been fatal. by the by, whenever our children or any of them are taken with putrid com-plaints, give them drink with acids, or according to the inclosed recipe, before you either give them cathartics or emetics, which do an infinite deal of mischief when prescribed too soon—knowing our Vessel, after a storm or two, to be a good sea boat, I was as easy in my state room (fixed in such a manner as not to be injured) in a gale of wind, if fair, as in moderate weather: I mean whilst we had sea room, for off the Scilly Islands,[2] I was uneasy and I think ye Captain was more so. indeed he said, "Should we be on a lee shore nothing could save us, the wind and sea were so high": This storm lasted three days & in eight or ten hours after it abated, we made land. this gale is mentioned in the english papers, as being very severe, according to the accounts received from all their seaports. at Torbay, the fleet under command of lord Bridport,[3] was generally dismasted. at Rams-gate, they have accounts of sixteen Vessels shipwrecked on the coast, amongst which were one or two packets, & it is further stated that the oldest person in the place had never recollected such a heavy sea. this was the opinion also of my captain, when he called me up to see it. I mentioned to you in one of my letters that we had nineteen days out of forty which were tempestuous; the last of these was off Rotterdam, a very difficult navigation—but what compleats this adventure, is the order issued by Monsr Cossin of Nantes, who has the general conduct of the privateers in that quarter, for them to cruize in the lattitude of the channel for the american ministers,[4] & to carry them to the West Indies, if captured. This he declared to Mr Peirpont[5] who was captured in an east Indiaman & carryed into that port very lately. Mr Peirpont is here, & gave me the information: & General Marshal confirms it, so far as this, that he spoke with a british frigate a little distance from the channel, who had just captured one privateer and was then in chase of another, the latter of which passed close to the Ship in which G Marshall was. indeed we would in all probability have been both taken, had not the General been saved by the frigate & myself by the british squadron* or the storm: in which case the W Indies would have been fatal to me, if not to both. Mr Peirpont is a genteel man, & is one of the house in New York who owns the Ship, said to be worth four hundred thousand dollars—on the 18th of Sept I arrived at Hellevert ?, on the 19th at night, at Rotterdam, on the 20th at the Hague, on the 21st at Amsterdam, on ye 22nd I returned to the Hague, on the 23d I waited on the french minister there & obtained a passport, on ye 24th I returned to Rotterdam, having in this little tour seen also Delft & Harlem. on the 25th in ye evening I embarked in a yacht for moerdyke [Moerdijk] on the 26th in the evening arrived at Antwerp. here I got a post chaise & having on the 27th had it put in proper order, continued my journey to Brussels where I lodged on ye 28th—on the 29th I lodged Alost [Aalst] the last city in Brabant, on ye 30th breakfasted at Gant a city in flanders & dined in Courtray another and passing thro Menin ye last city in dutch flanders at sunsett, I arrived at Lille in the evening. the next night Octr 1 I slept at Orché [Orchies] a frontier small city of france between Lille & Valenciennes & on ye 2d breakfasted at ye latter city. That night I slept at Cambray: on ye 3rd dined at peronne & lodged at Roye, on ye 4th dined at Senlis &

[13]

lodged at Paris. thus in 15 days from my landing, I saw about twenty cities besides some large & a number of small villages & travelled about 400 miles. my progress was too slow but my curiosity was for the time much gratified. since my arrival, my time has been principally occupied in receiving & paying the visits of americans, & making family arrangements. yesterday, being sunday, we according to appointment waited on the minister of foreign affairs with a copy of our letter of credence, & were received in an easy polite manner. Mr Tallyrand[6] the minister has been much misrepresented in the U States, his conduct having been very different from what was stated. he sent us this day cards of hospitality, and is to inform us in a few days what steps are next to be taken. I cannot at present form any idea of the final issue of our mission: but our reception, I think, is probable. this is all I shall say to you at present, my love, on politics: & you may impart it to our friends. Mr Foster is in Holland & I expect him soon in Paris. I had written him to come on, finding there would be no objection on account of his having been at London. the ministers of the U S are under one roof, have separate tables & families & carriages: & live sociably—everything is very dear here as well merchandise as provisions: manufactures from 25 to 40 per cent more than they were before the war.

I am extremely anxious to hear from you & our lovely children: God almighty bless you all; what would I not give to see & kiss you & them —the morning after my arrival I was waited on by the musicians of the supreme executive, & the succeeding morning by a deputation of Poissards[7] or fisherwomen for presents. Major Rutledge was kind eno' to negotiate for me, by which means I avoided the kind caresses of these ladies & an interview with the gentlemen. they expected a present of 15 or 20 Guineas, which each of us was obliged according to custom to give them, & when they (the ladies) can get sight of the ministers, as they did of my colleagues, they smother them with their delicate kisses. so much for the dignity of diplomatique bodies.

Where is Helen,[8] at New York or Cambridge? I can hear nothing of her, altho Vessels arrive from N York.

Let me hear, I beg of you, from yourself & the family by every opportunity: give my affectionate regards to our lovely children & Helen, & kiss them heartily for me: & be assured my dearest Life that I remain most sincerely & affectionately

Yours

PS from Amsterdam I sent by Capt Benjamin Ward in the brig Mary, a bottle of the Baume de Fioraventi & a letter. inclosed is a list of articles of bedding & cloathing returned by Capt Nutting.

* We ran thro the squadron in the storm off Scilly

NOTES

1. André-Simon Tissot (1728-1797). Born in Switzerland, he authored numerous medical treatises and in them set forth instructions for the treatment of ailments.

2. A small group of islands West by South of Land's End, Cornwall, the westernmost point of England.

3. Alexander Hood (1727-1814), 1st Viscount Bridport, and Commander of Great Britain's channel fleet.

4. The contents of this paragraph refute the oft repeated tales that Elbridge Gerry's voyage to France was marred by a fear of the Directory and that he "believed that they had ordered privateers to capture him and his colleagues . . . and send them to the Antilles." Samuel Eliot Morison, *By Land and By Sea* (New York, 1953), p. 192. The text clearly indicates that Gerry did not learn of this plot—if indeed the French had hatched such a plot—until after he arrived in Paris. Furthermore, his words make it plain that his informant, Mr. Pierpont, had received the story from a French naval official. Gerry himself jauntily notes "I have never enjoyed myself better" and very obviously relished the voyage, despite his sprained "ancle" and the distress he suffered from a serious infection.

5. Of Leffingwell & Pierpont, New York, owners of the ship *Confederacy*, Captain Scott Jenks, seized by the French while on a voyage from Canton to New York.

6. Charles Maurice de Talleyrand-Périgord (1754-1838), French diplomat, statesman and ex-Bishop.

7. Poissardes: fishwives of Les Halles, the public market in Paris.

8. Miss Helen Thompson, sister of Mrs. Gerry.

TO WILLIAM VANS MURRAY

Honble Mr Murray[1]
Minister resident at the Hague

Paris 9th Octr 1797

D Sir

I am favoured with yours of the 5th, & am glad to hear that Mr [Bossenger] Foster [Jr] is in Holland—inclosed is his Passport. I have not written to you, because I have nothing to communicate of importance. yesterday indeed we waited on the minister of foreign affairs & delivered a copy of our letter of credence. the minister received us politely, & in a familiar easy style. he signified, that in a few days he would communicate from the directoire, what steps we are to take next. I have been honored with a visit from the Poissards, but Major Rutledge was kind eno' to negotiate for me, & in my behalf to receive their affectionate caresses. I would have kissed them all to have promoted the object of our mission—I took both Lisle & Valenciennes in my rout & was much gratified.

10th I am informed this morning, that the minister at the Hague will be desired to give passport—

NB Mr Pierpont of N York, the bearer of this, has been lately captured in an indiaman belonging to his house said to be worth 3 or 400,000 dollars. . he appears to be a genteel man.

NOTE

1. William Vans Murray (1762-1803). Appointed by Washington minister to the Netherlands, he was, following the failure of Gerry, Pinckney and Marshall, appointed by President John Adams Envoy to France. In 1800 a second mission to France composed of Murray, Oliver Ellsworth and William R. Davies negotiated a treaty with Napoleon Bonaparte, the Directory having earlier been overthrown.

TO MR. BOSSENGER FOSTER, JUNIOR

Mr Bossenger Foster Junior

Paris 9th Octr 1797

Dear Sir

I am favoured with yours of the 4th, & inclose your* passport to Paris. I had written you on the 25th of Sept. from Rotterdam, & sent you a copy of the letter from this place. the original or copy you have probably received. your coming from London, is not considered by the minister of foreign affairs as a matter of any consequence. I expect to see you here soon & remain &c.,

* This you must receive from the french minister at the Hague.

TO MESSRS VANDERYUER, VILLEMONT & SCHWARTZ

Octr 8th 1797 Paris

Messrs Vanderyuer } 1
Villemont & Schwartz }

J'ai l'honneur de vous addresser, ci-incluse, une lettre de Messrs Willm & Jn Willink, & d'etre vos tres hum^ble & tres obeiss^t serviteur

NOTE

1. The Paris banking house handling Gerry's funds.

TO CAPTAIN EBENEZER NUTTING[1]

Capt Eben^r Nutting [of Boston]

Paris 10th Octr 1797

Dear Capt

This with a letter to Mrs Gerry, is inclosed to Mr Beeldemaker— the american Envoys have not yet been received by the Directory, but have had an interview with the minister of foreign affairs, who received them in a polite & friendly manner. This you may communi-

[17]

cate on your arrival at Boston, but I wish not to have it inserted in the papers, or to have my name mentioned—

NOTE

1. Master of the ship *Union*, which carried Gerry to France.

TO MR JOHN BEELDEMAKER

Paris 10ᵗʰ Octr 1797

Mr Gerry presents his compliments to Mr Beeldemaker & requests him to deliver the inclosed letters to Captain Nutting: or, if he has sailed, to send them in the first Vessel for Boston

TO WILLIAM VANS MURRAY

[The Letterbook copy of this communication is in the handwriting of Bossenger Foster, Jr.]

Letter to Mr Murray of the 31st Octr

Paris Oct 31st '97

Dear Sir

My last was by Mr Pierpont dated the 9th & no mention could be made of the rect of it in your Letters of the 10th & 13th—which have since arrived—but I presume that you have recd it ere this.

I am confirmed in my opinion at this time when I read the letter which you refer to, that it would be a subject of Altercation. is it not surprising that such letters which every one must suppose were not intended for the public eye should be published? be this as it may the publication of it is an unfortunate Circumstance & has a direct tendency to interrupt harmony with the Government which it respects. whilst this ought to be Cultivated & increased by every mean in our power—I think you were perfectly right in applying emollients—I hope they will Diminish the inflamation.—

The Dutch have been really unfortunate in the loss of so great a proportion of their navy—the Depressed State of that nation is not a pleasing consideration to my mind—

I am much obliged to you for your Case of the Letters & dispatches for Mr Adams, & for procuring a passt [passport] for Mr Foster.— the latter arrived here about a week or 10 days ago.

Your Letters to Mr Prince are sent forward—Gen Pinckney conceives as I do, that we have no authority to frank letters.

The Ministers of the U. States here are in a very unpleasant situation—they are not to be rec^d by the Directoire, & having no powers to negotiate upon certain propositions—*informally* made which the most extravagant imagination of any Citizen of the U. States could never have suggested. They expect every moment a formal hint to Depart & if made, will promptly obey it what the issue of this business will be I know not—but sure I am that France can promise herself nothing by a war with the U. States. she may indeed reduce them very low in the course of eight or ten years—by sacrificing a great number of her Citizens & two or three hundred millions sterling of her property but I think she can never Conquer them—& if she could of what benefit would they afterwards be to her—the fact is as I conceive it—that a small Cargo of Mexican Doll^{rs} would be more efficient in a negotiation at present than two Cargoes of Ambassadors.—

Pray present me in the most friendly terms to Mrs Murray & be assured Dear Sir

That I am yrs   Gy

Mr Murray Minister resident at the Hague.

TO CAPTAIN ALEXANDER ROSS

[The Letterbook copy of this communication
is in the handwriting of Bossenger Foster, Jr.]

Letter to
Capt A. Ross[1]

Sir   Paris 31st Octr – '97

I have rec^d yours of the 16th & have since heard that your Vessel & Cargoe are Condemned—it is grievous to the American Ministers to hear of the numerous depredations on our Commerce in violation, as we conceive of our existing treaty—but we can do nothing at present to prevent them.—We have been in this City nearly a month. are not rec^d by the Directors & are as distant from accomplishing the objects of our mission as we were on the day of our arrival—Should a negotiation however be opened, of which at present we see little prospect our first attention will be directed to the relief of our numerous unfortunate fellow Citizens—whose property has been sacrificed by the french Corsairs—& whose situation in this Country are truly Deplorable— with my sincere wishes for the Speedy & effectual relief of yourself & your Co-Sufferers I remain

Sir your very hble Servt

Gerry

Capt. Alex^r Ross

NOTE

1. A. Ross, to whom this letter is addressed, is probably Captain Alexander Ross "of Marblehead [Captain of a vessel not identified] taken by a privateer out of Bayonne [France] bound from Massachusetts to Spain with fish." *Quasi-War with France*, I, 23.

Ross, whose vessel was seized because she lacked a rôle d'équipage (or proper crew list), had in 1795 been given command of the ship *Hope*.

TO MRS. GERRY

Paris 4th Novr 1797

My dearest Life

I wrote to you a long letter of the 9th of Octr & sent it to Rotterdam to go by Capt [Ebenezer] Nutting, who was bound to Boston in the Ship Union; & from that time to this moment we have received no official communication from the French Government, & are in daily expectation of leaving Paris, without rendering any services to our country. I regret exceedingly, that matters are thus circumstanced; but see no remedy. not the least information can I obtain respecting yourself & ye family, & the want of it makes me very unhappy. I am obliged to conclude in haste with my most affectionate regards to yourself & the childn & all friends—

yours most sincerely

TO MESSRS JOHN & WM. WILLINK

Messrs John & Wm Willink
N & I Van Staphorst & Hubbard
of Amsterdam

Paris 6th Novr 1797

Gentⁿ

I have the honor of receiving your letter of the 30th of October, & have this day drawn on you a bill in favour of Messrs Vanderyuer Villemont & Schwartz for two thousand five hundred florins, holland currency. I drew the other bill which you mention, dated the 18th of Octbr for one thousand florins, when our friends Messrs Willink & Hubbard were in Paris, & for this reason, did not accompany the draft with a letter of advice—

I am &c

TO MRS. GERRY

Paris 28th Novr 1797

Mrs Gerry

I have written a long letter to you, my dearest life, but not having time to copy it, I substitute this line to inform you, that I am extremely anxious to hear from you & my dear children, not having recd a line or heard a word from you since I left Boston: & that my health is established since I arrived here. General Marshal & myself were badly accomodated in the house with General Pinckney, & at an extravagant price; we have new accomodations & elegant apartments at much less expence. We are not yet recd by the Directory; our situation is painful, but rather less so than it has been. I have no prospect that our mission will be of much service. God bless you & my dear children, kiss them all for me, & accept with them my most affectionate regards & fervent prayers for your health & happiness—adieu adieu—

TO MRS GERRY

By the Minerva Capt Sissons
from Havre   Paris 25th Nov 1797

Mrs Gerry

   Judge of my anxiety, my dearest life, when I inform you, that I have
not received a line from or heard a word of you since I left Boston.
letters are received from Boston New York & Philadelphia by Americans here, and also newspapers, but I cannot learn whether you & my
dear children are in health or even in existence. God grant that I may
soon receive joyful tidings[1]—as for myself, I am in good health at
present having changed my lodgings much for the better. six weeks
I lived in the same house with my collegues, with only a bed room &
parlour for myself, & antichamber for my servants. General Marshal
had just recd a suit of apartments, & both his & mine were badly furnished, not even having a carpet & being on the lower floor. my chim-
nies smoaked, & to compleat my happiness, there was a stable under
ground, in which there was a constant noise, as of persons breaking
through the wall, which at the same time that it disturbed my rest,
rendered it necessary to have a pair of pistols under my pillow. General Pinckney's rooms, which were on the second floor, were elegant
& commodious, & genteely furnished. thus circumstanced, I employed
a number of americans to look out for good apartments, & I have obtained them for General Marshal & myself, at Mad^m Villettes,[2] the
adopted daughter of Voltaire, at 12½ guineas a month, 5 guineas less
than we gave for those other inferior apartments. I have four large
elegant rooms for my suit on the second floor, which were occupied by
*Sir Robert Does when Ambassador from London, & chambers for
my secretary & servants. General Marshall has only three on the
Ground floor. Madam Villette is a widow lady of about 34 years old.
her husband [Charles-Michel] died about 4 years ago, at the age of
55, & left her a daughter who is now about 12 & a son about 4 years
old. she is to continue in the house during the winter, having an immense chateau, large enough to hold Genl Pinckneys family, in addition to those which now inhabit it. Madam Villette is I think one of the
finest women in Paris: on account of the goodness of her heart, her ex-

cellent morals, & the richness of her mind. She was the daughter of Voltaires particular friend, & lived with the former. he was charmed with her disposition & amiable qualities, & in his writings frequently speaks of her as the *belle* & *bonne*; by which name she is distinguished here. She was daughter of a Colonel in the Kings service, her uncle was a general officer, & her brother commanded the company which defended the queen, when attacked at Versailles, & lost his life at that time. the first notice which Madam Villette received of that event, was accompanyed with information that her brother's head & those of two other officers were brot on poles to Paris. her family was noble, & she married a nobleman, who was worth 10 or 12,000 louis, as it is said a year: but his extravagance had reduced her fortune to 2 or 3000 louis a year, & at the present time, this is still so reduced & she is so pressed for taxes, as to find it convenient to rent her house rather than to raise money at a great loss. this sacrifice of itself, shows that she has a great mind. she cannot do too much, she says, for her petites enfans. She speaks pure french & nothing else, which will be of great service to us. she is not handsome, but such a woman as you would like. my amusements have consisted in seeing the curiosities of Paris, Versailles, &c., in dining parties of Americans, & in attending the operas & theaters; for not the least notice has been taken of us by the directory or any officer of the Government, except by Mr Talleyrand, who has sent me a billet to dine with him tomorrow. at one time, I thot that appearances were very hostile, but they are not so at present, in an equal degree: altho I have not the pleasing prospect of our obtaining the great object of my accepting this appointment, a cordial reconciliation between the two republics. it is nearly three weeks since we wrote a conciliatory letter to the foreign minister, pressing an attention to our affairs, & requesting him to communicate it to the directory, but we are left without an answer, except that the minister Mr Talleyrand has communicated it to the directory.

I had forgot to mention an interesting subject respecting Madam Villette. soon after the death of her husband, & the birth of her son, she was committed to prison & put on Robespierre list of proscriptions —her little daughter, then about seven years old, insisted on going with her, & they lived together in the prison 10 or 11 months, she expecting every day to be guilotined. her fortune was her only crime, & it is highly probable that she would have been guilotined, had not the people of the Fauxbourg—where she lived, declared that she should not be injured, & that they would defend her. when she speaks of her daughter, it is in the most affectionate manner, always calling her la "petite charlotte". her health has been much injured by that event —her courage is unparellelled: what do you think of her ascending in a balloon,[3] soon after her marriage with two gentlemen & the daughter of one of them, & of her continuing in the air from 6 in the morning, till 2 in the afternoon? I have given you a particular history of this lady, without her suspicion that I have any information relating to her, & of my present situation, knowing it will gratify you to hear immediately how I am situated. she goes this morning to her Chateau, to arrange the affairs of her estate, & to bring her governess & petites. my lovely children, I flatter myself, & yourself are well: a line from you in confirmation of this, would remove a cloud, which for some time past has darkened my atmosphere. Decr 3. This evening whilst at dinner I recd a letter from my darling Catharine[4] of the 6th of Octr, with the joyful tidings that you had made me a present of a fine boy & was "about home". God be praised for this happy event. your apprehensions respecting it, your extreme distress when we parted, & my own anticipations, were sources of uneasiness to my mind, which can be easily conceived by you but not described by myself—poor General Fisk![5] the news of his death, notwithstanding his lingering indisposition, is distressing to my feelings. give my love to sister Fisk & the young ladies & inform them that I sincerely condole with them in the loss of so worthy a man & such a valuable friend.

Decr. 8th I have just recd a letter from Helen, which I will soon answer; give my affectionate regards to her & the children, kiss them all including master James Thompson[6] for me, remember me to all our friends & be assured that I remain—&c
Mr Foster is well & anxious to hear from his friends.

inclosed is a memorandum of articles sent by Capt Nutting. a bottle of the baume was sent by Capt Benjamin Ward in the brig Mary who sailed from Amsterdam ye latter end of Sepr last: & another by Mr Danforth son of Doctor Danforth of Boston who must have arrived there in Octr last three others were sent before.

* At this time Madam Villette resided at her chateau 30 miles from Paris where she has a large & valuable plantation.

NOTES

1. The "joyful tidings" which Gerry was impatiently awaiting was word from home announcing the birth of his fifth child.

2. Reine-Philiberte Rouph de Varicourt Villette, marquise de (1757-1822).

3. Historically this interesting account of Madame de Villette's balloon ascension is at once baffling, intriguing and frustrating. The first person to soar into the air was Jean François Pilâtre de Rozier who on 15 October 1783 ascended in a fire-balloon firmly anchored to the earth by guy ropes. A month later this intrepid individual accompanied by another equally stout-hearted companion rose 3,000 feet and remained aloft for 25 minutes in a free fire-balloon. Yet Gerry notes that Madame Villette's ascension took place "soon after her marriage," a ceremony solemnized 12 November 1777. A painstaking search of available records has so far uncovered nothing to substantiate this story. However, if this flight actually did take place, it may well be that Madame Villette was one of the first female balloonists in history, if not—together with her companion—the first.

4. Catharine Gerry, one of Elbridge's six daughters, later became the wife of James Trecothick Austin (1784-1843). A graduate of Harvard, a lawyer, and for a decade (1831-1843) Attorney General of Massachusetts, Austin authored the *Life of Elbridge Gerry* (Boston, 1828). Catharine, whose date of birth remains unknown, died 9 March 1850. With her mother, brothers and sisters she lies buried in the Grove Street Cemetery, New Haven, Connecticut.

5. Major General John Fiske (1744-1797), noted Salem sea captain and merchant. His third wife was Sarah Gerry, widow of John Gerry, Elbridge Gerry's younger brother.

6. James Thompson Gerry, his new-born son. Although the date of his birth is unrecorded, Catharine Gerry's letter suggests that Gerry's third son was born on the 5th or 6th of October, 1797. Appointed a midshipman in the U. S. Navy 20 December 1815, a year after his father's death, James Thompson Gerry rose through the ranks and was commissioned a Commander 17 April 1842. Fourteen years later, at age 57, he was lost at sea when his vessel, the 22-gun sloop-of-war *Albany*, carrying a crew of 210 officers and men, foundered during a severe storm.

TO MESSRS JOHN & WM. WILLINK

Messrs John & Wᵐ Willink
N & I Vanstaphorst & Hubbard

Paris 8ᵗʰ Decr 1797
24 Decr draw a bill for
ye same sum & write a
similar letter

Gentn

I have the honor to inform you, that I have this day drawn a bill in favour of Messʳˢ Vandynuer Villemont & Schwartz for twenty five hundred florins on your house, & that I remain &c

P S 24 please to indorse my account by the first opportunity.

TO A MR. PRINCE

Paris 10ᵗʰ Decr 1797

Mr Prince of Havre

Sir

General Pinckney having informed me, that you have kindly offered your services to forward our letters to America, you will much oblige me by sending the inclosed letters to Mrs Gerry by the first vessel for Massachusetts, or for any port not south of New York—

TO MISS CATHARINE GERRY

Paris 29ᵗʰ Decr 1797

Miss Cathⁿᵉ Gerry

a copy pr Capt Jackson to Mr Dickason[1] London
a copy by the Ship Lucy Capt [H. Joseph, of Philadelphia?] Dill
for Boston 11 Jany saild

I have received my darling Catharine your charming letter of the 23d of Octr, being the second which has arrived, & the warm affection which you express for your dear mamma & myself, I know to be truly

[26]

sincere, & it affords pappa the greatest pleasure. I am delighted to learn that your dear mamma is so well, & am sure that you will all make her happy as possible. the arrival of your aunt Helen, after my departure, must have been a great relief to your mamma, & would have made my mind more easy, had it been possible to have apprized me of it. I am grieved to find that dear mamma's eyes are no stronger, & inclose the advice of the best oculist in Paris. this I obtained of him, after having had a statement of your mamma's & your own complaints carefully translated into french by Doctor Swediaur,[2] the Physician recommended to me by Doctor Jeffries[3] & who accompanied me to the occulist Doctor Grand Jean I have also sent to Mr Dickason's father in London the same statement for the advice of Doctor Ware[4] whom Doctor Jeffries mentions as the best english occulist: & have requested him to send by different conveyances, four copies of his advice to your mamma. inform your dear mamma, that I will order some leeches to be sent from London, & some from this place: & that by writing to her sister Coles, some may be sent from Virginia. desire your Aunt Helen to write to Colo Coles immediately for some leeches. I am delighted to find that your brothers & sisters, aunt Helen & ye family as well as our friends in general, are well: tell my son Elbridge,[5] that pappa is charmed to find that he takes such good care of mamma & the family, & that he has been to church & behaved like a Gentleman: & desire master Thomas[6] also to be very polite to the young ladies & mamma & to take good care of them. . . .

NOTES

1. A London merchant with extensive commercial interests in New England.

2. François Xavier Swediaur (1748-1824). A prolific and popular writer, three of his medical books being published in the United States.

3. Dr. John Jeffries (1745-1819), physician and scientist of Boston. A Loyalist in the Revolution, Doctor Jeffries returned to England and with François Blanchard (1753-1809), made several balloon ascensions. They made one flight over London in 1784, and 7 January 1785 they crossed the English Channel. In recognition of this accomplishment, Jeffries was complimented by Louis XVI and dined with Benjamin Franklin at Passy. In 1790, Doctor Jeffries returned to Boston and soon established a large and profitable practice.

4. James Ware (1756-1815), English ophthalmic surgeon.

5. Elbridge, Jr. (1793-1867).

6. Thomas Russell (1794-1848).

TO MISS HELEN THOMPSON

Paris 3d Jany 1798

Miss Helen Thompson
a copy pr Capt Jackson to Mr Dickason
a copy Via Amsterdam

I have received, my dear Helen your two letters of the 27th of august & 7th of September, the first within a few days. I had received from my daughter one of the 6th of october, which gave me the joyful tidings of Mrs Gerry's being well abed. this interesting news did not arrive till the 8th of Decr, & the want of it distressed me exceedingly. it was not necessary for you to mention the attentions paid to your dear sister: I was sure of them, when I heard that you was with her. I have another letter from my dear Catharine of the 23d of october, which I have answered, the 24th of Decr. inclosed I send you the advice of the most famous oculist in Paris for your sister & her daughter: I have sent also a state of their cases to Mr Dickason of London, & requested him to obtain Doctor Wares advice, & to forward four copies of it to Mrs Gerry, & some leeches properly put up by an apothecary with each letter. I am happy to find that she is not in danger of losing her sight, & sincerely hope she will find a cure in the means now adopted. the two letters of my daughters before the 7th of Septr I have not received. I am delighted to hear, that all my lovely children are well, except my poor little Helen Marie,[1] for whom I feel distressed: Miss Catharine however informs me, she is better. God grant she may soon recover, & that in the spring I may meet my beloved family, of which I consider you as a part, healthy & happy. air & exercise are good for all ye children, & particularly for dear little Helen & my dear Mrs Gerry.

NOTE

1. Helen Maria, born 19 July 1796, died 7 April 1864.

[28]

TO MISS CATHARINE GERRY

(residue of ye letter to Miss Catharine Gerry 29 Decr 1797)

my darling daughter Miss Eliza[1] & Miss Ann[2]

I need not advise to be good, they are always so. poor little Helen Maria I hope is by this time perfectly recovered: air & exercise will be very good for her. & your little new brother I am sure will be a fine boy—the good conduct of the domesticks is a happy circumstance: & gives me great pleasure—your mamma is perfectly right not to trouble herself with relating domestic concerns, they will be conducted by her, better than by myself: but I regret the trouble she will have in these affairs—tell your dear mamma, that our negotiation is not yet commenced, & that we cannot rest much longer in this situation: that should we leave paris, I may possibly go to Italy, Switzerland & Germany, before I cross over to England: in which case she must not be uneasy, if my letters should not be regularly sent to her. adieu my dear, dear child, kiss dear mamma sisters brothers & aunt Helen heartily for pappa: give my most affectionate regards to them all & remember me in ye most friendly terms to all our friends in Boston & Cambridge &c being assured that I am

NOTES

1. Eliza, born in 1791, married David S. Townsend and lived ninety-one years, dying 2 May 1882.

2. Ann, born 22 December 1791, the same year Eliza was ushered into the world, was also blessed with longevity. She lived to reach the ripe old age of ninety-two, and is buried in the family plot in the Grove Street cemetery, New Haven, Connecticut.

TO MISS HELEN THOMPSON

residue of letter to Miss Helen Thompson   3d Jany 1798

I hope she has procured a wet nurse, this I consider as being essential to her health. I am rejoiced to learn that she supported her spirits. a depression of these under her circumstances, might have proved fatal to her. It gives me great pleasure to hear of our friends in Cambridge,

[29]

Boston Massᵃ & in general & N York: say to them all what you know or I would request you to say, if I had time to write of them in detail. I see no prospect of success in the embassy: we are not acknowledged, & it is not probable that we shall be: our residence therefore in Paris, will I fear be short. I have formed an acquaintance with several agreeable families here: & find their society charming. I was always fond, you well know, of the manners of the french, they are so hearty & sprightly & generous, as that it is impossible for me not to love their society. but the painful situation I am in mars all pleasure. the minister of foreign affairs, Mr Perigord Talleyrand, has been very civil & friendly to me. he dined with me a few days ago & sent me an invitation to a superb supper made for General & Madam Buonaparte: at which will be the Directory, all the foreign ministers, except the american Envoys, and the finest selection of ladies in paris. one of my colleagues urged me to accept the invitation. but it is impossible.

five bottles of Baume de Fioraventi have been sent as follows. one in July last by the Hebria bound for Havre to New York. another was carried to England, by Mr Wm Cutting of N York, who promised to send it from there. a third from Amsterdam by General Pinckney who probably sent a letter with it. a fourth by myself from Amsterdam the 20ᵗʰ of September, by the brig Maria Capt Benjn Ward bound to Boston: & a fifth by Mr Danforth son of Doctor [Samuel] Danforth of Boston, who must have arrived here in october last.

remember me most affectionately my dear Girl, to my dear Mrs Gerry & my lovely children & kiss them heartily for me. also to all our friends who may enquire for me.

P S Be particular in presenting my sincere regards to the Collector & our friends in that quarter; & to your family & all its branches at the southard.

TO MISS CATHARINE GERRY

By Mr [William] Lee, via Bourdˣ   Paris 10ᵗʰ March 1798
By Mr Dickason, via London

I have received, my dear & darling Catharine, your sensible & affectionate letters of the 8th & 23^d of Novr ye 2^d & 10th of dec^r & of ye 2^d & 15th of Jany.

on the subject of your dear mamma's eyes, I inclose Doctor Ware's advice, having before transmitted quadruplicates of Doctor Grand Jeans of this city. I am exceedingly anxious respecting them, & have written to Mr Dickason this day, to apply to Doctor Watham, another famous oculist in London for his opinion: conceiving that if the advice of one should fail, that another may succeed. I rejoice to hear, that her health is somewhat better, & hope it will continue to mend. you have not informed me what the matter is with her breast, whether the old or a new complaint.

The death of your poor Grandpappa, altho an event which I apprehended made me unhappy. your poor mamma will receive substantial consolation from the reflection that she has faithfully discharged her duty to him, whilst he was living.

I am grieved to hear, that my lovely little Helen Maria has not yet the use of her legs: to me it is a strange kind of affliction, & I wish to have the best advice on it. it gives me infinite pleasure nevertheless to hear, that she & all your brothers & sisters in general as well as yourself, are perfectly well. the air & climate of Paris agree with me perfectly well, & the society is charming but our political affairs wear a gloomy aspect.

I received a letter from Mr Dickason, a few days since, in which he expresses a hope of delivering your mamma Doctor Wares advice by the middle of the month. I wish I could accompany him. I expect however to embark, either from France or G B sometime in April or May. I cannot at present determine which: perhaps my next will give you the information.

I am sorry to hear that your cousin Lydia & Julia Knox are so indisposed, & hope as you are silent on the subject, in your last letter, that they are better.

I am glad, that you payed attention to my Captain: he conducted very well to me on the voyage. your attention to your musick & your dancing, & to your education in general, delights your pappa, as well as the accounts which you give of your lovely brothers & sisters.

[31]

tell Miss Eliza & Miss Ann, that they cannot conceive how much pappa is delighted with their conduct, & Master Elbridge & Master Thomas that they are gentlemen: & inform them all & Miss Helen Maria that pappa longs to see his darling Children & expects to find them the most charming little circle in all the state, & that dear little brother will play with pappa—I have not received the lock of his hair—give my affectionate regards to your Gr^d mamma & Aunt Helen & inform them that I sincerely condole with them in the loss of your Grandpappa. remember me in the kindest terms to all our Cambridge & Boston, Mhead & Salem Friends, Aunt Rachel Coles &c. I am happy to hear that the domesticks conduct so well; it will recommend them to my friendship—the winter with you I observe has been intensely cold, here it has been so mild, as that I have worn a muslin undershirt all winter, & now the trees are in bloom. kiss your dear mamma & all your dear sisters & brothers every day for Pappa, tell dear mamma that I am impatient to return to her & am determined never again to part from her: that happiness is only to be found by me in my family & with herself. give her & to all your brothers & sisters my most affectionate & tender regards & accept my dear & lovely child a full share yourself from your sincere & affectionate pappa.

P. S. Porter & every kind of small liquor, I am of opinion are injurious to your dear mamma. desire her, if she uses them, to leave them so as to ascertain the fact. the President, when he first went to Congress was obliged to give up the use of Porter, it almost made him blind.

inclosed is Doctor Wares advice, the same as you will receive by Mr Dickason. it will be delivered by Mr Lee of Boston (who married Miss Palfrey)[1] to whom you will pay friendly attention.

NOTE

1. Susan, daughter of Colonel William (1741-1780) and Mary Palfrey. Her father, a prominent merchant and patriot, served on the staff of General Washington. Appointed Consul-General to France in 1780, he was lost at sea when his ship disappeared without trace.

TO A DUTCH BANKING HOUSE

Messrs John & William Willink
N & I Van Staphorst & Hubbard
of Amsterdam.

Gentlemen   Paris March 13 1798

Your letter of the 22^d ulto. I have recd & have this day passed a bill on you in favour of Messrs Vanderyuer Villemont & Schwartz for two thousand and five hund^d florins, which please to honor & be assured &c. . .

TO MRS GERRY

By Mr Morgue   Paris 26 March 1798
Via Bourd^x

On the 10th of this month, my dearest life, I wrote a letter to my amiable daughter, & inclosed in it a copy of Doctor Warrens advice respecting your eyes; & I sent a copy of the letter to Mr Dickason at London; the original being sent by Mr Lee of Boston Via Bourdeaux

This you will receive by Mr Morgue a french young gentleman of this city, whose father was formerly minister of foreign affairs & whose family is very respectable. he has promised to deliver it himself, & will thus give you an opportunity of paying him attentions for his politeness—

My principal object is to inform you, that the minister of foreign affairs has in a letter which he has written to the american minister, signified the dissatisfaction of the directory at the conduct & disposition of my collegues towards France, & of their readiness to open the negotiations with me. this I have no power to do, & I shall therefore decline it: but another proposition is made, indirectly, that I shall remain here to prevent a rupture, which I am informed from high authority will immediately take place, on my departure. should this proposal be officially made, I cannot possibly decline it, because General Marshal & myself having made an offer about a fortnight past to the minister of foreign affairs to depart immediately for the United States & to leave General Pinckney here, & this not being accepted; if I should decline the measure, I shall be responsible or at least chargeable for the consequences. our object was, to lay before the government the true state of affairs between the two republicks, & to give it an opportunity of determining whether any & what further measures could be adopted to prevent a war. before I left you, I anticipated that this would be a painful enterprize, as you will probably recollect, but it has surpassed in this respect my utmost expectation. my collegues I have united with, in every measure which has been adopted: but their conduct to me has not been of that frank & friendly description which I expected. the whole of this, you will nevertheless consider as confidential. I shall soon write you again, whether I remain in or quit Paris, & with my affectionate love to my darling children & the most tender & sincere expression of it for yourself I remain your affect^{ne}

copy c/o Mon Florence
to Mr King
c/o Capt. Traill of Boston

TO MISS CATHARINE GERRY

by General Marshal   Paris 15th April 1798
extracts of Prince of the 2^d, 3^d & 4th para—

I received my darling Catharine about a month ago your charming letter of the 25th of august, & lately another dated the 19th of december.

Your dear mamma's eyes, I am distressed to hear it, continue weak. I presume she has received e're this Doctor Grand Jeans and Doctor Wares advice, the first being of this city, the latter of London: I have not yet procured Doctor Watham's, altho I wrote for it to Mr Dickason the 10th of march. it will be best I think to give each a fair trial, & to be fully convinced of the effect of the one, before the other is attempted. air & exercise ought to be particularly attended to, as they will invigorate your dear mamma & assist the prescription. malt liquors I suspect are very bad for the eyes, several of our friends have proved this by experience. a little porter & water now & then may not be hurtful.

I have a memorandum of the articles you mention, but I have no prospect of being able to go to England or Ireland before my return, altho I shall be mortified by the disappointment: the articles therefore which I intended to order from thence cannot be depended on, under existing circumstances. in my next I may give you better information.

I am extremely uneasy at the state of dear little Helen Maria's leg. it should be rubbed & brushed every day, & the muscles should be exercised by putting her on it: & to consult Doctor [William] Gamage & other good surgeons there is indispensibly necessary.

Inform my lovely son Elbridge that pappa is very proud of his son: that he behaves like a gentleman & that he must take good care of his dear mamma & the family: & my charming little Thomas that I am delighted to hear what a good boy he is & that I love him, brother Elbridge & his dear little brother & sisters dearly. Miss Eliza & Miss Ann I cannot praise too much, I am really too happy to learn with what propriety, delicacy & politeness they conduct themselves, & am very impatient to return & see all my darling children & their dear mamma. & you my charming Catharine I always think of with that warmth of affection which your attachment, tenderness & attention cannot fail to excite in the breast of your "dear pappa". I shall write to dear mamma by this conveyance: give my affectionate regards to her & all the children, with kisses in abundance & accept a full share yourself from your ever affect[n]

father   E Gerry

remember me in the kindest terms to all friends, not forgetting those at Plymouth: tell crasie & the family that I thank them for their expressions of friendship & wish to return & see them all as soon as possible—

[35]

TO MRS. GERRY

Paris 16ᵗʰ April 1798

copy by Mr Prince[1]
via Amsterdam—sent by him
from Bourdˣ to Phila

Mrs Gerry
    My dearest Life
    I have but a moment to inform you by General Marshal, that the executive directory have refused to treat with him & General Pinckney, but offer to treat with me. this has placed me in a most painful situation, for neither the government or the ministers anticipated such an event, & of consequence the former have not provided for it. the proposition I am not authorized to accept & therefore have rejected it: but it has been followed by another, that I shall continue here to keep up the communication untill our government can be informed of the state of affairs & take order thereon. I have been informed at the same time & indeed long before, officially, that if I should leave France an immediate rupture would be the consequence: thus circumstanced I am unavoidably prevented from fulfilling my intention of embarking this or next month for Boston, an object which of all others I most ardently wished for. unless which I yet hope for, I can persuade the minister to be reconciled to the measure indeed his consent will not avail, unless he can obtain the consent of the directory.
    It is uncertain for what Port General Marshal will embark: if for Boston I have informed him that I shall expect he will make head quarters at our house, with his Secretary Mr Brown & a young Gentleman Mr Gambol. in this event you will introduce him to Mr Macdonogh,[2] Mr Dickason, Mr Craigie, &c &c, I should have given him letters but he thinks there is no prospect of sailing for Boston
    adieu my dearest life, God almighty bless you, our lovely children & family as well as all our friends. kiss the petites for dear Pappa &c.

Mr Foster went to London about ten days past: Mr Farwell of Virginia is now my secretary.

TO MRS. GERRY

Paris 20 April 1798

Mrs Gerry

This you will receive, my dear life, by citizen Giraud,[1] Consul of France for Boston. he was formerly a member of the french Convention, bears a respectable Character & as far as I can judge from one or two interviews, justly merits it. I need not suggest the proper attentions.

My collegues have left Paris, General Marshal to embark by the first Vessel for Bordeaux, & General Pinckney to spend some time in the South of France, for the recovery of his daughters health.[2] I made a proposition in our last conference with the minister, [Talleyrand] that General Marshal & myself should embark on the first vessel, we having before agreed on this arrangement; but the government would not accede to it, & informed me that a rupture would be the consequence of my leaving France, whilst they expressed a wish that the other gentlemen would depart. I am extremely anxious to return to you, as I fear that your additional cares in my absence, will be too much for your health. indeed there can be no advantages, but infinite disadvantages from my remaining here longer, than to afford the government an opportunity of proposing a plan of accommodation. I hope this will be done, that it will be liberal & magnanimous, & strike dumb those enemies of both republicks who wish to embroil them & who by a contrary policy would be triumphant.

Give "dear pappa's" affectionate regards to his lovely children, kiss them all for me & be assured my dearest life of the most sincere & affectionate attachment.

1. Marc-Antoine Alexis Giraud, Commissary of Commercial Relations, Boston, Mass., for the states of New Hampshire, Massachusetts, Rhode Island and Connecticut.

2. In a letter dated 19 June 1798 Abigail Adams, the wife of President John Adams, informed her sister that "Mr. Pinckney is gone to the South of France with a persuit for the Health of a daughter suposed in consumption." Stewart Mitchell, *New Letters of Abigail Adams* (Boston, 1947), p. 193.

TO MISS CATHARINE GERRY

Paris 24 April 1798

Miss Catharine Gerry

I have received, my dear & darling Catharine, within three or four days, your charming letters of decr, 4th, 25th, Jany, 5th, 11th, 19th, & 21st Feby.

It is a happy circumstance to me, that the letters communicating the indisposition of your dear mamma the misfortune of hurting her breast, & the dangerous accident of running a pin into her foot, informed me of her recovery. her danger was great from the last accidents. I lately pricked a tendon of my finger & altho I kept it in brandy two or three hours during the day, two days afterward I was taken ill at the table with a sickness at my stomack & general indisposition. I immediately applyed oyl of turpentine to the wound & in half an hour felt better, but did not recover untill the fourth or fifth day, my former health. in case of such accidents always apply it, & prevent the wound from healing soon.

The deaths of your poor Grandpappa & cousin Lydia [Knox] & the indisposition of your Grandmamma, aunt Helen & our family increase my anxiety to return. the state of health of your Grandpappa made it reasonable to expect the painful event which your letter communicated, but your cousins health was such as to have left me unprepared for this melancholy news. if your Grandmamma & aunt Helen will stay with mamma, I doubt not it would be of service to them.

You complain of the want of letters—since that by Capt Nutting, I have wrote the following to yourself, mamma & Aunt Helen ye

1 Novr 4–

1 Novr 25 by Capt Sissons from Havre

1 Novr 28–

1 Decr 29 Sent to Mr Dickason at London

a copy——by the Lucy Capt Dill of Boston

1 Jany 3 to Mr Dickason

a copy—sent to Amsterdam } for Aunt Helen

1 Mar 10 by Mr Lee of Boston

a copy—to Mr Dickason

1 Mar 26 by Mr Morgue

a copy sent to Mr King at London

1 April 15 by Gen¹ Marshal

a copy—by Mr Prince, Boston

1 April 16 By General Marshal also

a copy   by mr prince

a April 20 by Mr Giroud now french Consul for Boston

I wrote your Aunt Helen as follows ye 3ᵈ of Jany "five bottles of
Baume de Fioraventi have been sent vizt, in July last by the Hebria
bound from Havre to N York   1 by Mr Wᵐ Cutting of New York
who promised to send it from England. a third from Amsterdam by
General Pinckney. a fourth by myself from Amsterdam the 20ᵗʰ of
September by the brig Maria Capt Benjⁿ Ward bound to Boston. a
fifth by Mr Danforth Son of Doctor Danforth of Boston, who must
have arrived in October"

inclosed is a letter to Colo Pickering to supply dear mamma, if necessary, with money.

I hope dear little Helen & your uncle Gerry will soon have the use
of their legs: the loss of the use of Helen's is a serious matter & re-
quires the best advice. your uncle's gout will probably leave him in
good health.

I will be careful to have stores in plenty whenever I embark, & I
hope it will not be long before this desirable event; I shall use every
effort to make my proposition of departure agreeable to the Directory,
for if they should still be against yᵉ measure, I must remain here to
prevent an immediate rupture.

[39]

I am happy to learn that your little brother thrives so well: kiss him, dear mamma, brothers & sisters heartily & give to all of them who can understand you my most affectionate regards. being assured my dear child that I remain with the most tender attachment, your truly

affectionate parent

Sent to Mr Dobre
copy by Capt Worsely

TO MR TIMOTHY PICKERING

Paris 25th April 1798

Timothy Pickering, Esq.[1]
Secretary of State of the U States

Dear Sir

If Mrs Gerry should have a demand for money before my return, which I flatter myself will be soon, please to answer her bills to the amount of two thousand dollars or any part thereof, which she may judge necessary. I have the honor to be Sir, &c.

Sent to Mr Dobre[2]

NOTES

1. Timothy Pickering (1745-1829), Revolutionary War general and statesman, born in Salem, Massachusetts. On 10 May 1800, he was summarily dismissed from his post of Secretary of State by President John Adams because of his anti-French attitude and his political manipulations.

2. P. F. Dobree, U. S. Consul at Nantes.

TO MRS. GERRY

Paris 30th April 1798

Mrs Gerry

I have just received, my dearest life, a letter from Mr Dickason, the father, containing Doctor Wathams advice, a copy of which is inclosed. No person can be more attentive & obliging than Mr Dickason has been in obtaining the advice; & speaking of Doctor Watham he says that "he is, most certainly, as an occulist second to none in this kingdom & is retained by the royal family." Mr Dickason will send some leeches under the particular care of Capt Traill of the mendiant of Boston. kiss our lovely children for Pappa & be ever assured of my most affectionate attachment

P. S. I am in hopes of embarking for the U States in all June or the beginning of July. I have wrote to London for all the articles you have desired.

Sent to Mr Dobre
Copy to Mrs Dobre

TO MRS. GERRY

Paris 15th May 98

In addition, my dearest life, to the preceding I have the pleasure to inform you, that I shall certainly sail in the Sophia,[1] [Capt. Henry] Geddis, some time in June.[2] I hope to have the pleasure of seeing you the latter part of July, or what is more probable the 10th or 15th of August. Kiss our lovely petits &c.

To Mr Dobre
copy with Mr Wathams advice
for Mr Deblois to Bourd^x

NOTES

1. A 12-gun United States navy transport.

2. Despite Gerry's high hopes, the *Sophia* did not sail until the second week of August.

TO MISS ELIZA GERRY

Paris 12th July 1798

Miss Eliza Gerry

My darling & affectionate Eliza has written a charming letter to Pappa of the 10th of march, which has really surprised him. the letters are well made & put together, the words are handsome & above all, the sentiments & information are delightful. I inclose advices of two more eminent* oculists of Paris, to cure dear mamma's eyes. She

[41]

must try but one at a time, & wait to see its effects. I am very sorry to learn that my darling children Catharine & Helen are not well: the blisters evidently injured the eyes of the first & must never be repeated. desire dear mamma to try several times the points of highly polished scissors[1] on Helen's legs & the sole of her foot, lightly, perhaps it may assist her. inform dear mamma that I have been ready to leave France five or six weeks, but cannot obtain a passport. The Government of France is desirous that I should treat, but I have no powers; they have desired me to remain and to send for them. I have answered I cannot do this & my return is indispensible. but notwithstanding that I cannot obtain the documents, vizt the passport &c, although baggage has been on board the State's brig Sophia several weeks. tell dear mamma not to make her mind uneasy about it, for if a war was to take place, my person would be as safe here as at Cambridge. kiss dear dear mamma, sisters, & brothers for pappa, give his affectionate regards to them all & accept a full share yourself from your truly affectionate pappa.

P. S. I have sent duplicates of the advice in a letter this day written to dear catharine, by another vessel, & shall bring with me the drugs directed by the occulists, lest they may be scarce in America.

France will not declare war now; its Government says it wants with the United States peace.

July 15. I have the promise of my passport &c, & expect to embark by the 25th of this month.

* Wenzel & Demours

NOTE

1. The "scissors" Gerry recommended Mrs. Gerry use on their daughter's legs and the soles of her feet were probably Perkin's "metallic tractors" or a similar contrivance. These instruments, devised by Elisha Perkins (1741-1799), a physician, were utilized by him in an ingenious attempt to apply to medical practice the principles of the discovery of Luigi Galvani (1737-1798), who had demonstrated that electric current produced by galvanic action would cause muscles to flex and reflex. This phenomenon was promptly seized upon as a method of relieving bodily ills. To bring about a "cure" the "tractors" were alternately drawn or stroked over the affected limbs or regions of the body.

TO MISS CATHARINE GERRY

Miss Catharine Gerry

My dear & darling Catharine is I hope better than when she wrote her letters of the 10th, 15th, 20th & 27th of march & 11th of April. I have been detained here a long time by the publication of our dispatches & the detention of my passport, but have the prospect of obtaining it soon & of sailing the latter end of this month. I shall therefore be as laconic as possible. inclosed is the advice of Damours & also of Wenzel, two more celebrated oculists here: let each of them have a fair tryal: but finish with one, before the other is commenced, & see the effect of his prescription. desire your dear mamma to be particularly attentive to this. I have written to my dear little Eliza, & desire that you may desist from following Grand Jeans advice, & that helens legs with ye soles of her feet may be lightly passed on by points of high polished scissors; & have in her letter sent duplicates of the advice. The drugs prescribed by the oculists I shall bring with me. your particular history from time to time of the family concerns have been the greatest source of pleasure I have had here. may the health of your dear mamma, yourself & sister Helen, who was a lovely infant before her sickness, be restored & the health of my other dear children be confirmed & continued: & may pappa soon meet you all perfectly happy. kiss most affectionately for pappa, your dear dear mamma, Brothers & sisters, presenting to each my sincere & ardent love & accepting a full share of it yourself—adieu my dear darling Catharine

> your affectionate
> pappa

I have this morning recd the promise of my passport & expect to embark about ye 25th.

TO MRS. GERRY

Mrs Gerry

Inclosed, my dearest life, is a memorandum of the sum which I have drawn since my arrival here on Messrs John & Wm Willink N & I Vanstaphorst & Hubbard Bankers of the U States at Amsterdam, amounting to twenty one thousand six hundred florins of Holland. this sum was paid into the hands of my bankers here, Messrs Vanderyuer Villemont & Schwartz of whom I have received it without addition. I have also drawn for my secretarie's salaries but am not chargeable for them. I shall leave Paris tomorrow, to embark at Havre & expect to arrive about ye middle of September in America.[1] adieu my dearest love, kiss our lovely children heartily for Pappa & be assured with them of my sincere & ardent affection for you all.

NOTE

1. Gerry departed Paris the day after he wrote this letter, leaving the affairs of his country in the hands of Fulwar Skipworth [1765-1839], U. S. Consul at Paris. A fortnight later, on 8 August, the *Sophia* weighed anchor, and after a voyage of two months landed Gerry at Boston 1 October 1798.

* * * * * * * * *

[The following communications are written into the back pages of Elbridge Gerry's Paris Letterbook. The first, second and third are addressed to President John Adams, the fourth and fifth to Mr. Thomas Jefferson. They fill completely both sides of pages 40-85 and are introduced by an explanatory marginal note which reads "Copy of letter press sheets fading out by time." By comparison, the penmanship of these transcripts indicate that they were copied by Ann Gerry, the daughter and first born child of Elbridge and Ann (Thompson) Gerry.   R. W. K.]

TO PRESIDENT JOHN ADAMS

Cambridge 5th July 1799

Dear Sir,

In your letter of December 15th, referring to General Marshall's journal, you are pleased to observe "that my *Seperate*, and *secret* conferences with Talleyrand, & my advocating a stipulation for a loan to be paid after the war, will do no good to me or to the public; & that Pinckney & Marshall will attest to the correctness of this journal, & will be believed."

My conferences with Mr Talleyrand were on the 28th of October, & 17th of december 1797, & the 4th, 5th, 6th, & 7th of Feby, & 1st of March 1798: these were all my conferences with him, previously to the receipt of his last letters to the envoys; beside them there were several attempts of Mr Talleyrand which failed. on the 30th of Decr when he dined with me he proposed the 5th of January for an interview: I called on him, & he was with the directory he afterward appointed the 20th I attended, & he was with the directory. again he proposed the 24th, I went, waited some time & finding him much engaged left the office without seeing him. the 2d of Feby was then mentioned I called, & he was not at his office. on the 3d he sent his secretary to me, we agreed on the 4th, & then met.

If my conferences are complained of, because they were *seperate*, the other envoys were the *cause thereof*. in the dispatches of all the envoys, of the 8th of November 1797, it is stated, "that Gen'l Pinckney, & General Marshall expressed their opinions, that not being acquainted with Mr Talleyrand, they could not with propriety call on him; but that according to the custom of France, *he might expect this* of *Mr Gerry*, from a previous *acquaintance in America:* This Mr Gerry reluctantly complied with "& again on the 30th of December, when Mr Talleyrand as before stated, expressed a wish to see me on the 5th of January, in order to make some communications, I noted the particulars, & soon after imparted them to my colleagues, informing them "that the conference, proposed by Mr Talleyrand was a measure which I could not accede to, unless sanctioned by them; that if they concieved no injury could result from it, & that it may give the envoys some information which might be useful, I would meet the Minister otherwise I must decline it let the consequences be what they may to myself; since good intentions are not all that is expected of negotiators, who are often calumniated, for measures truly meritorious." these were my words to the other envoys, & they sanctioned the meeting—every attempt to meet the minister, between the 5th of Jany

& the 2^d of Feby having failed, I wrote a line to General Pinckney, informing him, that it was again proposed I should call on Mr Talleyrand on that day, & that I wished to confer with him & General Marshall on the subject he answered by letter marked A. of the date: we all met &, I desired the other envoys to express their opinions on the subject, because if they tho't it best I would excuse myself immediately: or, if not, I wished to know how to conduct in case of new propositions. we all agreed, that I ought to go & were decisive against a loan, on my return that day from the Bureau, without seeing the minister I met him near General Pinckney's hotel whose foot man attending me, & knowing Mr Talleyrand, stopped my coachman, & informed me, that the minister, had just passed on his way to the Bureau. but wishing not to see him I ordered my coachman to stop at General Pinckneys & informed him that "I had escaped an *interview* than *which* nothing could be more disagreeable to me."

On the 1st of March the last of the days of the conferences mentioned, the Secretary of Mr Talleyrand calling on me said that the minister wished to see me. I waited on him, & he stated that Mr Rutledge had delivered him a letter from the American ministers of the 27th of February, requesting an interview, & that he had appointed the 2^d of March for the purpose, but that he would confer with me on the subject, if I preferred it then.

I answered no, I preferred a conference in company with my colleagues. I wished however as we were together, he would think of a proposition, which I then made vizt that he should give us his ideas of the general principles of a treaty, such as France desires, & I would propose to my colleagues, that we should return him a counter project. but he declined it instantly, saying, it would give the directory unnecessary trouble: that if the proposition of a loan was adjusted, every thing else would be accomodated without difficulty; & thus we parted —every thing that passed at these interviews, except those of the 4th, 6th, & 7th of February, relative to my treating seperately, was immediately communicated to the other envoys; & the October & December conferences were published.—It must be evident then, that if any blame results from my conferences, because they were *seperate* it attaches to my colleagues.

[46]

With respect to the conferences which were *secret*, they were the inevitable consequences of those which were *seperate*. On the 4th of February, when Mr Talleyrand informed me, that he had something of vast importance to communicate to me, it was impossible for me to derive what it was, or whether it respected the United States, their government, the envoys, generally or myself in particular. the first reflections which occurred to me, were, that either the impediments to our being accredited, would be communicated, & knowing them, the envoys would be able to remove them: or that this was an artifice of the minister, to obtain from me the refusal of his proposition of secrecy, & then to charge me, with having defeated the negotiation; in either view of the subject, it was necessary to consent to secrecy. the principal secretary of the minister's bureau, had on the 30th of Decr when they both dined with me, declared that he tho't it would be impossible to reconcile the directory of Gen'l Pinckney that it would be acting the part of a good citizen to remove the obstruction by quitting France, which he could justify to his Government, & that then General Marshall & myself may carry on the negotiation. I told him instantly, this was impossible, & he shrugging, dropped the subject. all which was the next day communicated to the other envoys, & I did not expect ever to hear such another proposition.

The proposition of secrecy did not relate merely to my colleagues, as has been represented by Mr Pickering, it was general: & they were immediately informed, that proposals of an extraordinary nature had been secretly made to me, that I should communicate them, when at liberty to do it, & that in the interim, they may be quite easy, for that I had rejected them. but on the supposition, there had been on foot, a stratagem, for causing, by false information, an arrest of all or any of the Envoy's; or which was not impossible, that they were in danger of being massacred; or that such an attempt on their government was, contemplated; or that by a deep artifice, it was intended to encrease the animosities of the two republics against each other, & to produce a declaration of War; what could be said in justification of a minister who had refused confidential information for defeating such measures; & if none of them had existed, it might have been said they did exist, & that I refused amicable means for counteracting them. numerous other circumstances might have rendered unwarrantable, a refusal of information, merely because it was confidential. indeed I believe, no minister ever did, or ever would, refuse it under such circumstances; for no injury did, or could possibly result from the secrecy of my conferences, & advantage might have been taken of a refusal, to throw the blame of a War on the American Government. it must be evident, therefore if any imputations results from the secrecy of the conferences, it also rests on the other Envoy's, who gave rise to them.

Since your return Sir, you have informed me, if I recollect rightly, that General Marshall in his journal has stated, that I advocated a loan generally. but I cannot think he meant this, as there was not the least pretext for such an assertion. it would be such a flagrant violation of truth, so directly contrary to all the documents of the embassy, & to my well known conduct in France, as to induce me to suppose he never intended to make such an impression. it would indeed be repugnant to his own conviction, & to common sense. for he knew, that in regard to the War between france, & Gr Britain, I considered the United States in many respects as being embarked with the latter; that I concieved the overthrow of her Government, as involving that of our own; that I was ardently desirous of preserving peace, on just, & honorable terms, with all the belligerent powers' & wish none more so than with G. Britain; & that I was always of opinion, a loan to France during the War, would immediately involve us in one with G. Britain. I shall only therefore consider, what is quoted from your letter, "that my advocating a stipulation for a loan to be paid after the War, will do no good to me, or the publick" & that Pinckney, & Marshall will attest to the correctness of this journal & will be believed." I know very well, that when parties run high, as they lately have in the U. States, each is disposed to believe its own advocates, & this often in opposition to conviction itself. but every candid Man, I think, will believe the facts I shall state, confirmed as they are by my general conduct, & opposed as they will be to the gloss, & color, of art, & sophistry.

On the 25th of February Mr Talleyrand, by his Secretary, desired I would consult the other Envoys, & inform him, whether we would consent to a loan after the War; this he said had never been before proposed, or, on the part of the U. States objected to; & if we would meet Mr Talleyrand on his ground, he would propose it to the directory; but could not say, what their opinion would be on the subject. I informed him that the measure had never to my knowledge occurred to any of us, that I could not say what would be the result, but that in compliance with Mr Talleyrand's request, I would communicate it to the other Envoy's, as I did on the evening of the 25th & in a long conversation, General Pinckney & General Marshall expressed their opinions to this effect:

That it was not certain the proposition if approved by us would be acceptable to the directory, as they know nothing of the matter.

That the proposition, if made by us, would be a surrender of our Independence.

That we had no powers, & that such a loan would not be acceptable to our government or ratified by it.

That if adopted, it would produce a civil war.

That it would in effect, be a loan for the war, because on the faith of its stipulation money would be borrowed & applyed to the War.

That the object of that government was not to form a treaty, but only to amuse us, till the event of the expedition to England could be known,

and, That they were averse from any more informal negotiations.

They were therefore for rejecting the proposition mentioned.

In regard to the first point, I was of opinion, that any measures, if wise, & salutary, which should be adopted by us & rejected by the directory, would place them in the wrong: but that if a measure of an opposite nature should be rejected by us no disadvantage could arise from its being also disagreable to the directory. moreover, that there could be no doubt the proposition was from Mr Talleyrand, as it came thro' his confidential secretary, the only person admitted in some of my secret conferences with the minister: & that the probability was, Mr Talleyrand would not have ventured to make the proposition unless he had consulted the directory: but therefore that the certainty or uncertainty of the directory's conduct on the occasion, ought not to affect our decision.

The second objection, relative to the surrender of our independence being involved in our making such a proposition, appeared to me novel, the proposition had been made by Mr Talleyrand, as a ground of accommodations & he considered it as an act of reciprocity for the loan made to us by France, that if we had power, it was a meer question of policy, whether we should accede, or not accede to the loan, which determined in either way, would not be a surrender of our independence, or in any degree affect it. that even the offer by us of such a loan, which was not proposed, would not so much wear the aspect of an involuntary act, as our consenting to one if proposed by the directory; but that the mode was of little consequence, & I presumed would be so considered by the directory. that I was as much averse from every kind of loan, as either of my colleagues; but that having to deal with a government, which regarded power, more than principle, the question was, which of two evils was the least, a loan when peace should be established, or the hazard of a War? that if our Government had given us powers to make such a loan, they had decided this point; otherwise the decision rested with them. that in the latter case, I was for stating the matter to our Government, & for giving it an opportunity to grant, or refuse the power; & I offered immediately to return to America, if the other Envoys would remain at Paris! and to propose, if the power in question should be granted, that another person should be sent in my stead, or that they should finish the treaty.

In regard to the third point, that we had no power, & that such a loan would not be ratified by our Government; my opinion was, that our powers were ambiguous. the Envoys were particularly instructed in regard to the claims of our citizens "not to stipulate that they should be assumed by the U. States, as a loan to the french Government": & also "That no aid be stipulated in favor of France, *during* the *present War*." but as there was not a word in the instructions respecting a loan after the War, it was not manifest, from them, either that the Government would object to, or sanction such a loan if adopted by the envoy's as a necessary measure of accomodation, & altho the last mentioned instruction "that no aid be stipulated *during the War*" might by some be viewed in the light of a negative pregrant, and be supposed to imply that such an aid might be stipulated *after the War*, it nevertheless appeared probable to me, that had our Government contemplated a loan after the War, mention would have been made of it. I regretted my not having been able to see the President, & receive information on this head, & several other's, & concieved that our powers, & instructions ought to be well examined. that if it should appear we had power to make such a loan, we had no reason to doubt if adopted by us of its ratification by our Government, & that if we had not power, we ought not to assume it. in a subsequent conference, General Pinckney enquired of me, whether, if I was negotiating, I would agree to a loan after the war, & I answered no, I would not without further instructions.

In regard to the 4th point, a civil war, my opinion was, that if a loan to take place with peace, should be proposed to us, & our rejection of it should bring on a war with France, it would tend more to produce a civil war in the U. States, than the consent of our Government to such a loan. it appeared to me, that our citizens having claims for 20, or 30 millions of dollars, would in the event of a war, lose the prospect of recovering them, & impute the loss to the refusal of an act of reciprocity, as the proposed loan was called. they & the citizens in general might suppose that our Government could not have lost much, if any thing, by lending france after the war; 5, 6, or even 10 millions of dollars; that if notwithstanding the immense resource of France, there was any risque from such a loan they would calculate it & consider the loss of a million or two of dollars in this war, as trifling compared with the incalculable evils resulting from a war. amongst these they would probably class, the loss of 20, or 30 millions of dollars due to our citizens, an additional public debt of 2, 3, or 400 millions of dollars, a ruined commerce, violent political parties, & injuries not to be repaired in half a century, indeed all that we said in regard to this, on either side was but conjecture.—with respect to the 5th point, that a loan to take place with the peace would in effect be a loan for the war, I observed that in case of such a proposition, even if our powers should be deemed adequate, & the measure eligible, I could never consent to it unless expressed in such terms as to preclude the possibility of negotiating the loan during the war. that it should contain an express condition to be null & void should it hereafter appear that such use had been made of the stipulation before the peace, & that on these terms I would never consent to such a loan, unless it became part of a treaty, in which all our just claims should be established, as well as other matters relative to the negotiation.

In regard to the 6th point I concieved that whatever our sentiments were, we ought not to conduct on the principle, that the french Government was insincere in its proposals for peace; because this would preclude all negotiation, & we never could agree on any terms, that the french Government could have no object in amusing us, during her expedition against G. Britain, because the U. States, if immediately at war with France, could not assist Great Britain so as to effect the smallest degree, the expedition against it. and if revenge was her object, she might pursue it against the United States, after the issue of her expedition against the british was known, as a peace, or conquest would probably be the result unless a new coalition should be formed against France that if the United States, in case of a war, contemplated a defensive or any other treaty with G. Britain, this should be formed before the commencement of the war, for after it, the motive on the part of G. B. would be diminished, that should they form a treaty to their wishes with the british government, necessity or the plea of it, may produce a seperate peace, as in the case of the late coalition, & we ought therefore to calculate our defence, on our own resources. that of these the Government was the best judge, as well as of the policy of accelerating, or retarding the war, and that if the directory means to amuse us, we ought so to conduct, as to make their intentions manifest.

With respect to informal negotiations, I stated my aversion from them. that they had been to me a source of vexation, & trouble. that this was a proposition directly from the minister by his confidential Secretary which I was desired to communicate to them, seeing they had not met Mr Talleyrand themselves, & that in doing this, I had discharged my duty.

On the 26th Mr Talleyrands private Secretary called, & said the minister entertained hopes that we should meet on the ground of a loan after the war, & enquired, whether I had conferred with my colleagues on the subject, & what was the result? I answered yes, & it did not appear to us, that our powers were adequate. he was struck with the information, changed color, & said "then I fear the matter is at an end." in the evening I communicated this to my colleagues, & we agreed to send in a letter to the minister requesting a conference. General Pinckney then desired to know whether, when we had seen Mr Talleyrand, I would sign the letter requiring our passports. I answered, that I could better determine this after the interview, that we were sent to make peace, &, I was determined not to quit the object, whilst there were hopes of accomplishing it. that the proposition of a loan after the war was a new one, & this interview would probably inform us of the nature of it. General Marshall wished to know, if the minister should state a proposition of the kind mentioned, what answer we were to give him, & said, he & General Pinckney were decidedly for an answer, that we had no powers;—I told him, I chose to consider the powers thoroughly before I gave this answer. that we might say to the minister, this being a new proposition should be considered by us, & that he should soon receive our answer. General Marshall said, that he, & General Pinckney, forming a majority had a right to determine the question, I replyed that if they were desirous of giving the answer they proposed immediately, I would not object to the measure provided, they would take on themselves the responsibility of their decision: but that it was a matter of such moment, & our powers on this head were so equivocal, that I would not risk a war, which might turn on this answer, without a further view of the subject. Genl Marshall then stated a supposition, that Mr Talleyrand should not mention a loan after the war, but for the war, I answered, that this point was unalterably decided, we had agreed not to listen to it, & showed him the measure was impracticable, he then stated another difficulty, if a loan was proposed after the war, how could we ascertain, whether it was intended to be used for raising money before the peace; seeing we could not make this enquiry without compromitting ourselves, to accede to a loan after the war, if not so to be used. I answered, I did not wish to compromit him, or myself, either, that we might draw from Mr Talleyrand, an explanation, if requisite, of his proposition in various ways, one of which might be by saying we understood it, to be a loan not to be used in any way directly, or indirectly, before the peace: & I further observed, that there did not appear to be much difficulty in ascertaining his object without compromitting ourselves in the least. we then drafted the letter to Mr Talleyrand for a conference, & parted.

That letter was followed by two conferences, between the Envoy's, & minister, & a suspension by us all, of our letter demanding passports: it being stated at the conclusion of the last conference, which formed a part of our despatches, "that two of us would return immediately to receive the instructions of our Government, if that would be agreable to the directory; if it was not, *we would wait some time in expectation of receiving instructions*."

And here, it may be necessary to remark, that on the evening preceding the 22ᵈ of Feby when General Marshall & myself had agreed to visit Madam Villette, at her country seat, he informed me, that the letter to Mr Talleyrand, demanding our passports, was ready, & proposed that we should sign it, & leave it with General Pinckney. I answered, that this was an unexpected proposition, that he knew we had engaged to go the next day to *Villette*, 30 or 40 miles distant, that on delivery of that letter to Mr Talleyrand, our passports would probably be sent to us, with an order to depart immediately, that my baggage was unpacked, & my bills were unpaid, that a day or two, at least would be requisite for these matters, but that I would send an apology to Madam Villette, would prepare immediately to leave the City, & would then sign the letter. this he declined, & preferred a postponement of the signature till our return. soon after this, the proposition of a loan was made, to take place at the peace.

It may be proper, further to remark, that the Envoy's after their first conference with Mr Talleyrand of the 2ᵈ of March, met, & the question being, what answer we should make to him on the 6ᵗʰ,—the time proposed for our second meeting of him, I made this proposition, which was agreed to, delivered by Gen'l Pinckney, in my words, & published in our despatches, vizt.—"That we had considered with the most serious attention, the conversation we had the honor of holding with him, a few days past; that the proposition he had suggested appeared to us to be substantially the same with those which had been made, by Mr X, & Mr Y, & also to Mr Gerry with an intention that they should be communicated to his colleagues. that we considered it, as a proposition that the United States should furnish aid to France to be used during the present war, that altho' it was unusual to declare instructions, yet we would declare to him, that in addition to its being a measure amounting to a declaration of war against Great Britain, we were expressly forbidden by our instructions to take such a step."

From these facts it must be evident,

That I was uniformly, & decidedly against a loan during the war, for these amongst other reasons, that it was expressly against our instructions, & would amount to a declaration of War against G. Britain.

That it was impossible for me to have advocated a loan after the war; because our powers being ambiguous, it did not concieve we were authorized to make it. for this reason the ambiguity of our powers, I was against an affirmative, or negative answer to the proposition for a loan, or a declaration that we had or had not powers; if to be avoided, that my object was, to refer the question of the loan after the war to our Government for decision, & by the mode of doing this, to prevent a war; or if it should take place, to deprive the directory of any pretext, of its being more disposed than the Envoys to a reconciliation.

That I was ready to sign the letter for demanding our passports, when it was first proposed, on condition of my being indulged a short time, a day or two only, to prepare for departing from France, but that when the proposition was renewed in the midst of our debates relative to a loan after the war, I was for postponing that letter, until we had finished the matter before us, & that finally we all agreed to postpone the demand of our passports, in expectation of recieving instructions.—this I presume will expose some unfair insinuations, said to have been made, in regard to my not signing the letter for passports.

It will be observed that I was particularly attentive in France, to measures for preventing national divisions, or an increase of them. Unanimity I considered, as a rock of salvation, because if by diplomatic artifices, a quarter, or third of our citizens could be rendered dissatisfied with the administration, it would so distract & weaken our public councils, & operations as to render us an easy prey to our enemies; against whom, our wanted unanimity could always oppose an effectual barrier.

Having lately recieved from Mr Pickering a statement of my account, & thinking it in several instances, unjust, I shall submit it, with some remarks thereon, to your consideration in a few days.

I have the honor to remain Dear Sir, with every sentiment of respectful attachment

Your most obedient, & most humble servant

E. Gerry

His Excellency
Mr Adams President
of the United States

TO JOHN ADAMS, PRESIDENT OF THE UNITED STATES

Remarks on General Marshall's letter of the 12th of Nov., & Mr Pickerings of the 10th of December 1798 to Mr Gerry; respectfully submitted by the latter to the President of the United States of America.

1st. In regard to the source of information (relative to the renewal of one or both the money propositions) which General Marshall thinks, I must have supposed to be him: I had not the means of ascertaining it: nor could I suppose it to have been either of the other Envoys, for in that case, I should have had a right to expect, the information would have been correct.

2ndly. General Marshall "knows not why, I supposed the publication" in question, "a stigma to myself"; & thinks "it contains nothing indelicate, or with which I have a right to be displeased". his reasons are "that it was not stated, to have been in my power to have avoided the application," " nor was it insinuated that I approved or received it favorably," "that I was not censured, for not having made the communication to Government"—"nor could he have intended such a censure, since he himself must have participated in it." that I did not withhold the conversation (vizt of X & Y relative to the money proposition) from my colleagues." "& that it was nearly as incumbent on him, as on me to have suggested the propriety of mentioning it to the Secretary of State." "that it was deemed unnecessary" by the envoys: & that this fact (the renewal by X & Y of the money propositions) would not have been brot into view, but in consequence of the astonishing impudence, manifested by Mr Talleyrand, in demanding of me, the names of W, X, Y, & Z." but, without any of these qualifications, or explanations, & at a time when prejudices, ungenerously, unjustly, artfully, & cruelly excited against me in my absence, and without any friendly advocate, had taken deep root, & threatened the destruction of myself, & family, that publication was made in the words following:" But there is one important fact relative to this business not mentioned in the dispatches from the Envoys, which ought to be universally known, and of the truth of which I have incontrovertable evidence, it is this "the company at the private (this word & some others following were italicised) dinner to which Mr Gerry was invited by Mr Talleyrand, consisted of X, Y & Z. after rising from the table, X & Y renewed to Mr Gerry, in the room, & in the *presence* (tho' perhaps not in the hearing) of Talleyrand, the *money propositions*, which the Envoys had rejected! & yet Mr Talleyrand has affected ignorance, who were meant by X, Y & Z! what unexampled effrontery!—let any candid man, Sir judge whether this clause "contains nothing indelicate" in regards to myself; Whether "I had not a right to be displeased with it", or whether "it was not a stigma on me". can any one, Sir, say, that "if the company at the *private* dinner," consisted of Mr Talleyrand, X, Y, Z, & myself. it had not the appearance of a clandestine meeting, for the purpose of intrigue, & of my having been the cause of its not being "mentioned in the dispatches" & "universally known". & can any one assert that this was not the impression which the publication had a tendency to make? & that "the effrontary of Mr Talleyrand "unexampled" as it was, would not, *at my expence*, have been heightened, had the company consisted, only of the five persons mentioned: can any one, considering the conduct of Mr Pickering in general towards me, & particularly in this instance, doubt of his intention to make that impression? & can any one say that "the company at the private dinner to which Mr Gerry was invited by Mr Talleyrand, consisted of X, Y, & Z", or that the former was not warranted in saying this "important fact never existed". I shall be loth to make any observations in the distinction of General Marshall between "official, or publick" & "private dinners". they are to the President, I am sure unnecessary.

3ʳᵈˡʸ· General Marshall states, as a wonder of wonders, that I should deny "the fact itself". but he did not state the fact, which I did then, & do still deny, that the company at the private dinner, to which I was invited by Mr Talleyrand consisted of X, Y, & Z: & which he admits I have a right to deny; for he says that *he does not recollect* to have heard me mention any more than X, Y, & Z, and the *Secretaries*, who are the family of Mr Talleyrand". the fact of which I was doubtful Vizt whether X & Y renewed one or both of the money propositions is by General Marshall substituted for the one which I denyed, & which "never existed". in regard to this fact, I think now, from the best of my memory, as I then tho't, that the proposition for the loan only was renewed; but if General Marshall thinks he is correct in his statement, that according to my information to him & General Pinckney "X & Y made a repetition of the money propositions", be it so, it is a matter of no consequence, further than that I wish for an accurate statement of facts. if he has not mistaken my information the fact was as he has stated it.

4.thly. The company consisted, not only of Mr Talleyrand, X, Y, Z, & myself, & the Secretaries, but also of Mr [Richard] Codman, who came to the lodgings of General Marshall, & myself, to accompany me to the dinner; a circumstance which he has undoubtedly forgot; & of Mr [Fulwar] Skipworth, & many others.

5.thly. General Marshall had undoubted evidence, that I supposed, as well as himself that X, Y & Z were well known to Mr Talleyrand, he knew that I drew the first paragraph of the last conference of the Envoys with Mr Talleyrand, in which they informed him that "the propositions he had suggested, appeared to them the same, with which had been made by X & Y, & also to Mr Gerry, with an intention, that they should be communicated to his colleagues;" & he admits, that "I expressed a good deal of indignation, at the renewal of one, or both the money propositions. he ought therefore to have manifested a disposition, to have removed from the public mind, the possibility of an imputation to me, in regard to the events.

6.thly General Marshall has expressed a wish "to save us both the pain of an altercation". he knew how earnestly I wished to avoid this, & what I had suffered to prevent it: but he had no right to expect, that I would permit the publick to be poisoned by injurious & unjust suggestions, & implications against me, without correcting them.

7.thly Mr Pickering states, his having informed the President, that he could not publish my letter (which he says seems to have been proposed as the means "to do myself justice") without subjoining some remarks which might wound my feelings. he "seems" to have taken some exceptions to that letter, because proposed "as the mean" to do myself justice. I made no such proposition, nor had such intention. on the other hand, you know well, Sir, that I wished for the matter to be so corrected, as to prevent injury to the feelings of any one: but Mr Pickering must have had the fibres of an anvil, & supposed that I had the same, to have conceived, that his letter to Mr Johnstone, or his report to the President, had not wounded my feelings. I wish

[59]

never to wound the feelings of any man, but, confess that it has been with great difficulty I have refrained from doing myself public justice. (nothing but the Presidents request, & an aversion from interrupting the publick tranquillity, which is remarkable, & I am informed has been promoted by the publication of my dispatches, have prevailed on me to endure ungenerous & unmerited reproach.)

8^{thly} Altho' Mr Pickering in his report alluded to, stated what he had omitted in his letter to Mr Johnstone "that when the money propositions were renewed" Mr Gerry very justly offended answered positively in the negative, & the conversation dropped". yet he has not corrected his misrepresentation that I dined in company consisting of Mr Talleyrand X, Y, & Z, & has moreover repeated his uncandid remarks in regard to my giving Mr Talleyrand the names of his agents.

TO PRESIDENT JOHN ADAMS

Remarks of Mr Gerry on Mr Pickerings report communicated to Congress on the 21st of January 1799 respectfully submitted by the former to the President of the United States.

There being nothing in the Constitution, or laws of the U. States, which authorises a Secretary of State to superintend a public minister, & the report referred to not being predicated on any general or special injunction of the President to Mr Pickering, his animadversions on any part of my conduct, relative to the embassy are an unprecedented assumption of power; which is not, & I concieve ought not to be entrusted to a Secretary of State: inasmuch as it tends to confound the authority of the supreme executive with that of its organ of communication the Secretary, to embarrass, controul, & even defeat, its measures in regard to negotiations, treaties, & foreign connections, to degrade, & debase the office of a minister, & to subject him to dark intrigues, unmerited reproach, & the highest injustice; But had the report been official, it is in many respects unfounded.

1st Mr Pickering after stating that Mr Talleyrand on the 30th of

[60]

May prayed Mr Gerry "immediately to make known to him the names of W. X. Y, & Z. observes that Mr Gerry in his answer of the 31st" wishes to evade Mr Talleyrands request, & with reason for he, & his colleagues had promised X, & Y that their names should in no event be made public.—if this paragraph was meant to insinuate, that Mr Gerry did not keep his promise, it is unjust; & it is difficult to concieve for what other purpose it was merited.

The despatches of the Envoys of the 22d of October 1797, conclude with this clause, to which Mr Pickering refers "the nature of the above communication will evince the necessity of secrecy, & we have promised Messrs X, & Y that their names shall in no event be made public. if this clause as it respects myself as to be considered in its full sense, which is questionable, it expresses in strong terms, 1st "The necessity of keeping the despatches secret. & 2dly a promise obligatory as the Government, concieved on itself, as well as on the Envoys, that the names of X & Y should on no event be made public.

With respect to the first altho' in the opinion of the Senate there existed a necessity for the publication of the despatches, this nevertheless promulgated information which rendered me particularly obnoxious to the directory & its minister: it subjected the Envoys to suspicions of having carryed on criminal intrigues with X, & Y, & of having promised for that reason to conceal them, it produced on the part of the directory, an unqualified demand of me, as an act of justice of the names of X, & Y, publickly announced as their accusers. & it tended to bring on an immediate rupture between the two republics: of this there can be no doubt, for I was well informed that in consequence of the publication the question of War with the U. States was warmly agitated by the Directory, & negatived by a majority of one only.

In regard to the 2d point, it is evident that on presumption the despatches would have been secret whilst any of the Envoys were in France, the promise was on a great measure founded. this I affirm to have been the fact as it respected myself, & it would have been folly in the extreme for the Envoys, on the presumption, or probability, that the despatches would have been published whilst they were in

[61]

France, to have pledged themselves not to make public the names of men, who as the Envoy's so late as the 8th of november acknowledged had not produced a document to prove they were empowered even by the minister to hold any communication with them: or in other words to prove they were not intriguers.

It might be further observed that those intrigues as they were called, & the publication of them were considered by the Government of France, as an outrage against it, & as an evidence of an intention to disaffect its citizens, & stir them up to sedition.

Judge then Sir of my situation, obnoxious as I was thus rendered whilst in the power of that Government & of the reasons furnished by the publication of the despatches, for the dispensing with the promise had I indulged the inclination.

But what was the promise? & how on my part has it been performed? the promise was to X & Y that their names shall in no event *be made public*. it cannot I presume be said, the promise implied that the names of X & Y should not be made known to the Directory, if demanded. the Envoys could not have promised this, without considering X, & Y as intriguers against the french Government, & themselves in the same light; for why conceal their names from their own Government if it had employed them? moreover, the refusal of the names, on condition they should not be published, would have been unwise, if X, & Y were its agents: by thus furnishing the Directory with a pretext for disavowing them, & with the stronger argument for throwing an odium on the Envoy's: unwarrantable, if they were not its agents, by concealing their names, & unjustly imputing their guilt to the Directory: & on either case the refusal might have been disgraceful to my Government as well as myself, by subjecting its minister to be dealt with as an intriguer.—neither can the promise of the Envoy's be supposed to extend to their Government, without charging them with a violation of it, at the moment it was made, or charge, which altho' unjust, is more plausible, than that I made a breach of the promise because the communication of the names to their Government by the Envoys, necessarily extended to a Senate which have found it difficult, if not impossible to keep a secret, &

which was under no express obligation to keep it, whereas my communication was made under a promise of secrecy to the most impenetrable cabinet of Europe. the promise was nothing more or less than that the names of X, & Y should not be notorious, or generally known which is the true definition of the word "public" as applied in this case. it must be evident then that the promise on my part, under every embarrassment, has been faithfully kept, that it has been more than fulfilled, inasmuch as the names of W, & X are still secret, & those of Z, & Y, had they not announced themselves, would have been so likewise, altho' there was no promise of secrecy to W. or Z.

I cannot forbear remarking in this place that from the beginning, I was apprehensive of disagreable consequences from those disgraceful conferences, and had the measure which I proposed, as early as the 21st of October to the other Envoys, been adopted the negotiation would have terminated differently. the copy of that proposal was inclosed to Mr Pickering in my letter of the 24th of november in the words following, "To the question whether the proposition, informally, & confidentially communicated to us as private citizens, at the request, as is stated of Mr Talleyrand in his private capacity, will be adopted as the basis of a treaty? this answer is given that it is highly probable, some of the propositions communicated on the evenings of the 19th & 20th of October (being the 28th & 29th Vendemiaire) will be considered as the basis of the project of a treaty, & others as inadmissible, but that it is impossible to discuss them, or come to a decision on them; until they are presented to us in our official characters." at the bottom of the original of this proposition now in my possession, is written in General Pinckney's hand writing, "intended to be given Saturday the 21st of October." And Sir, had the Envoys been charged, as they undoubtedly would have been in case of a war on the evidence of their despatches, with an intention of stirring up the french citizens to sedition, there was not the least proof as will hereafter be shewn that X, & Y, or any other person was authorized by the directory to propose to be Envoys a douceur or any corrupt measure, & it will also appear that this evidence of such authority from the minister was feeble. indignant then as the directory was at the charge of corruption, it would not have hesitated to condemn the Envoys for having carryed on intrigues & provoked the publication of them for seditious purposes: & how disgraceful would have been the consequences. *Burlamaqui* Vol. 2ᵈ—Chap. 15. Section 12 says "With regard to Ambassadors who have rendered themselves culpable, either they have done the injury of their own head, or by their masters order, if they have done it of their own head, they forfeit their right to security, & to the enjoyment of their privileges when their crime is manifest, & heinous." "by *heinous crimes* are here meant, such as *tend* to disturb the state." "when the crime directly affects the state, whether the ambassador has actually used violence or not, that is to say, whether he has stirred up the subject to sedition, or conspired himself against the Government, or favored the plot, or whether he has taken arms with the rebels" & "we may be revenged, on him even by killing him not as a subject, but as an enemy." "but if the crime be committed by the master's order," "we may in this case secure the promise of the ambassadors till the master shall repair the injury done by the Ambassador, & himself."

2ᵈˡʸ Mr Pickering asserts that I certified to Mr Talleyrand the names of his own private agents! & if he means that the object of the certificate was to inform Mr Talleyrand of the names of his agents, it is not a fact. it appears from the anonymous publication No. 35, & from other parts of my communications that the certificate was given to Mr Talleyrand not in his private capacity but as minister; and not for the information of himself, but of the executive directory which required other evidence than his, of the names of the intriguers & demanded it of me. but the propriety of my having given the certificate is I presume so well established as not to admit of the least doubt.

3ᵈˡʸ Mr Pickering states, "that besides certifying to Mr Talleyrand, the names of his agents, I *added*, "that they did not produce to my knowledge credentials or documents of any kind." & herein he again misrepresents the fact—it will appear by my letter to the french minister No. 12, that the names were certifyed *without any addition whatever*. my previous letter to him No. 7 contained this paragraph which

[64]

is *partially* quoted by Mr Pickering Vizt. "If any of those persons (alluding to the intriguer)" were unauthorized to act, or, having definite powers have exceeded them, they certainly have abused this government, & the Envoy's likewise: but I am incompetent to judge of these points, as they did not produce to my knowledge credentials or documents of any kind." I was here writing of the french government, not of its minister; Mr Pickering seems to consider them as synonymous terms, but the Government is as distinct in my mind from its minister, as the pen which the latter directs is from himself; & I declared my incompetency to judge of the conduct of X, & Y, because they had not produced to my knowledge either credentials or documents. And was it ever pretended, that the intriguers did produce credentials or documents of any kind from the directory? on the other hand, did they not expressly declare to the Envoys "that they were clothed with no authority whatever"? but if Mr Pickering wanted any other evidence than the paragraph quoted, to prove that it had no reference to Mr Talleyrand, but related merely to the Government, he might have found it in the next paragraph of the same letter, wherein I informed Mr Talleyrand "that the publications referred to (Vizt. of the despatches) are sufficient to show the delicate situation I am in with respect to the names of the persons, & are marked with such circumstances as to enable him to investigate the subject without insisting on any communications on my part." herein I pointed to my conference with him of the 28th of October & 17th of December, as being sufficient for him to ascertain the names. the two paragraphs, the first mentioning the french Government, & not the minister & asserting that the intriguers had produced no credentials, or documents from it, & the other mentioning the minister, & not the government, & suggesting that he knew the intriguers are so remarkably expressed, as not to have left a possibility as I concieve, of any persons applying what was said of the Government to the minister, or of what was said of him to the Government. Mr Pickering, after thus distorting my meaning, goes on to assert, that the declaration of Mr Talleyrand to me Vizt. "that the information Mr Y, had given me (on the 17th of December) was just, & might always be relied on" "stamps with the ministers au-

[65]

thority, all the communications made by Mr Y to the Envoys." let us now enquire, whether there is any foundation for this assertion? Mr Y states, at the time mentioned "that two measures, which Mr Talleyrand proposed being adopted a restoration of friendship between the republics would follow immediately, the one was a gratuity of £50,000 sterling, the other, a purchase of thirty two millions of the dutch rescriptions—immediately afterwards, we met Mr Talleyrand at his Bureau, & I informed him that Mr Y had stated to me that morning, some propositions as coming from him, respecting which I could give no opinion. Mr Talleyrand in answer said, "that the information Mr Y had given me was just, & might always be relied on "*but that he would* reduce to writing his propositions which he accordingly did", & "the substance was as follows "That the Envoys should come forward generally & say, France has been serviceable to the United States, & now they wish to be serviceable to France, understanding that the french republick has sixteen millions of dutch rescriptions to sell, the United States will purchase them at par, & will give her further assistance, when in their power". from these facts omitted by Mr Pickering, it appears that after I had informed Mr Talleyrand generally "that Mr Y. had stated to me some propositions as coming from him," & after he had said in answer, without my specifying the propositions "that the information Mr Y had given me was just, & might always be relied on." *he explained himself;* saying, "*but that he would reduce his propositions to writing;*" which he immediately did, & they related on the part of the United States merely to the purchase of dutch rescriptions, & to their giving France further assistance when in their power—a question arises then whether after Mr Talleyrand had thus qualified his declaration, respecting Mr Y's information to me, that declaration was to be construed in any other, than the qualified sense of the person who made it? if so was he not precluded from the right of explanation, universally admitted to every person, whilst speaking? & moreover, was not his meaning ascertained by a general expression, altho' he instantly explained, & limited it by writing? but if the declaration was not to be so construed then Mr Pickerings assertion is altogether unfounded, "that this declaration stamps with the ministers authority, all the communications made by Mr Y to the Envoys." or that Mr Y, produced to me any credentials, or documents whatever from the directory, or even from Mr Talleyrand which authorizes his proposition of a douceur. so far was that declaration from being a credential, or document, or evidence of either, for Y to propose a douceur, as that it was an *evidence to the contrary*. but if the written explanation of Mr Talleyrand was a nullity; & his declaration to Y a document from himself, yet, to consider it as a document from the government is, as I concieve the height of absurdity.

4ᵗʰˡʸ Mr Pickering, in considering Mr Talleyrands declaration to me —"that by offering money we could prevent the effect of the arretté" of the directory for rejecting the Envoy's, states, that "this matter of money could only refer to the douceur." but, whatever it referred to, it appears in itself as a proposition to mulct the President, for his daring to exercise a constitutional authority, rather than as a douceur: more especially as it was in *commutation* of the proposed explanations, & reparations, be this as it may, it can neither be considered as a credential or document to X, or Y from Mr Talleyrand, much less from the Government, which is what I contend for.—the same may be said of Y's declaration, that he had Mr Talleyrand's orders for what he said, or did; for admitting the fact he did not produce them to me, or any other person, to my knowledge. neither can an argument be urged from the similarity, of language between the french minister, & X, & Y, in regard to the douceur, & the irritation of the Directory for the latter was communicated to us before we saw X, or Y, & was a subject of common conversation. & X declared to the envoys, that "there was not an american in Paris, who could not inform us, that nothing was to be obtained of the french Government, *without money*. as to Mr Z's urging a douceur to Mr Trumbull, I never heard before Mr Pickering's report, that he had suggested the measure to any one. he certainly never did to me. all Mr Pickering's reasoning's therefore on the subject, may have the weight any one is disposed to give them; for establishing a bad opinion of the Directory, or its minister, but they have none to invalidate in the least my as-

[67]

sertion that the intriguers, so called, did not produce to my knowledge credentials, or documents of any kind from the french Government.

5^{thly} Mr Pickering has stated but *one* pretense (for selecting me) which was, that "my opinions, *presumed* to be more impartial, promised in the course of the explanations, more of that reciprocal confidence, which was indispensable." & he has considered the objectionable opinions of my colleagues, as being relative to the embassy. whatever was presumed of my opinions, no person, at that time, except the envoys, knew any thing of them, in regard to the embassy, other than what was expressed in the despatches: & therefore no comparison could possibly be made between our opinions if different in this respect. but there were other pretenses than the one mentioned. Mr Talleyrand, as is stated in my letter to him of the 20th of July, & 24th declared to me that "the opinions & conversations of my colleagues had produced embarrassments, & dissatisfaction on the part of the directory, & its determination not to treat with them." he was informed of some of those *opinions*, & *conversations*, which were communicated to the directory, & did not relate to the embassy. whatever were my opinions relative to the embassy, I carefully avoided uttering, or writing any of them in regard to France which could offend either the french Government, or people: & when mixed with french citizens, I treated them with attention, & common friendship. if this conduct, or the preference, or presumption, it actually produced, is considered by Mr Pickering as a subject of censure, it was nevertheless authorized, & enjoined by the law of nations. Vatel[2] Book 6 Chap. 7.—sect. 93 says "as to the prince, to whom he is sent, the ambassador should remember that his ministry, is a ministry of peace, & that on this footing alone he is recieved. this reason interdicts every evil practice to him." speaking ill of the french nation or Government, would have been an evil practice, & I was justified in avoiding it. decency likewise requiring a reciprocation of attentions, & civilities, I could not dispense with them.—some letters of the other envoys, were also intercepted. what their contents were I know not, but we were all alarmed on the occasion, & tho't it best to conceal our papers; lest

[68]

a general order for seizing them, should be the consequence, indeed it was generally understood that the opinions which rendered the other envoys obnoxious in France were irrelative to the embassy, & fraught according to the french representations, with prejudices against the french Government, & nation. nothing therefore can be more injurious, unjust, or contrary to well known facts, than any insinuation that the disposition of the directory to treat with me, was the result of my not having as invincible a determination not to surrender the honor, the interest, or the independence of my country, as either of my colleagues.

6^{thly} Mr Pickering asserts, that "unfortunately Mr Gerry was induced by the threats of immediate war against the United States, to separate from his colleagues, & stay at Paris. threats, which viewed with their motives merited only detestation, & contempt." that "four or five months before, the threats of immediate orders to quit France, & the terrors of war, in its most dreadful forms, had been held up to all the envoys," & that "those threats had not been executed." but let me enquire, by whom were the terrors of war, & threats held up? by the minister? no, but by individuals, without a credential or document to prove their authority. the declaration, respecting an immediate war, which induced me to remain at Paris was *official*, from the french minister, & in the name of the executive directory: circumstances which did not leave a doubt that the measure would take place, when it was considered, that France was then in the Zenith of her power, at peace with, & counted by all Europe, except G. Britain; in alliance with Spain, Holland, Switzerland, & a great part of Italy, in the midst of the most formidable preparations to invade G. Britain, and in the practice of carrying all her declaration officially made, into immediate effect. had I by quitting France, under such circumstances, bro't on a war, the measure would probably have produced, in the United States, a clamor even from some who would have rejoiced at the event, & might have exposed me on the principles of the Constitution, & laws of the land, to an impeachment. & would the law of nations have warranted such conduct? Puffendorff book 8, Chap. 6, Sect. 11—says "It may be further enquired, whether a *pre-*

fect, or *Governor*, who hath *no general*, or *particular* commission to warrant him, can justly make *War* upon a foreign *State*, or *Prince*, only upon, *presumption*, or because he believes his *Sovereign* will approve his *action*? which, in my opinion, must be denied. for it is not sufficient to know, what it is *probable* his Sovereign would approve, if he were consulted in such a particular posture of affairs; but it should rather be considered, *what it is probable he would desire should be done without his advice*, when the matter will bear time, & the point is nice, & difficult, if a law were to be made upon it, where he must determine universally of all such cases. and then no doubt it will appear, that it would be provided that no *minister, should undertake any action, in which the Commonwealth is nearly concerned* (such as a War is, & especially the offensive which is the proper subject of the present enquiry, & which will, generally, well enough admit of delays) without the advice of his *Sovereign*. and therefore, tho' it should happen that the *Sovereign* should, at the same time think *a War* with a certain Enemy *necessary*, yet, to be sure, he cannot be pleased to *see his minister* go beyond the bounds of his duty." altho' this paragraph is predicated in a prefect, or Governor, it is equally applicable to every Officer of Government, & is actually applied by the author to *Ministers* in general. & altho' it is predicated of offensive war, he also applies it to War generally: & conceives that if even the Sovereign thinks it *necessary*, he cannot be pleased with his minister, who without his advice, has involved him in *a War*, by going beyond the bounds of his duty. And would any minister of common prudence, in my situation, without knowing the sense of his Government on the occasion, or recieving a line of information from it for seven, or eight, months have risqued the plunging it unprepared in any respect for aught he knew into a war with the most formidable Nation on Earth; rather than have enabled it, by the earliest information, to prevent, & whether this was possible or not, to prepare for the event? moreover, had I manifested a disposition to depart, it probably would have produced an arrest of all the Envoys, a seizure of their papers, as was the case with the Portugueze minister on a similar occasion, & the anathemas' of my fellow citizens for such a rash step. it is an easy matter to fault ones

[70]

conduct by sophystical means, on any occasion; but difficult to conduct rightly, under numerous embarrassments to which I was continually & unavoidably subject, at Paris. to add to them, at the time when my duty prompted me to remain there, I would have given half my property, to have returned to my Family, from which I had recieved the most distressing information.—But, my stay at Paris, is said to be unfortunate. What I expressed in my despatches, as a probable measure, has actually happened. nearly all the powers of Europe, not in alliance with, or under the control of France, are at war with her. and is it a misfortune, that the United States are preserved, from the most horrid conflict, that was ever known? had I left Paris, with the other Envoys, war without doubt, would have been the consequence: & this was not only suspended by my remaining there, but it will probably be avoided. events have proved it then to be, not an unfortunate, but the most fortunate circumstance that could have happened: for no one could then, or can now say, let the issue of the European contest be what it may, that it will not produce such a political state of affairs, as to call forth all our resources for defence, or, if these should be previously squandered by an unnecessary war, to render us liable to foreign domination.

7^{thly} Altho' on the 14th & 18.th of October 1797, the informal negotiations were commenced by an American Officer Mr W & Mr X with one of the other Envoy's, & on the 21st of October, I made a proposition to them for terminating those disgraceful measures, which have been justly disapproved by the President of the United States, Mr Pickering, carefully avoiding the least stricture on my colleagues, & on the other hand paying them the highest compliments on every occasion, has concealed from the eye of the public that proposition, & used his endeavors to excite the publick indignation against my conduct.

8^{thly} The partiality of Mr Pickering's conduct is still more manifest, in regard to the much "talked of" douceur, inasmuch as the Envoy's, when it was proposed by Mr X "told him, that if we could see in France, a temper sincerely friendly to the United States, we might not regard a little money, *such as is stated to be usual*, altho' we should

[71]

hazard ourselves by giving it." & they, in answer to Mr Y's propositions of the 30th of October, say, that no diplomatic gratifications can *precede* the ratification of the treaty. I am content to bear my proportion of blame, in this respect, altho' I did not make the declaration, or propose the answer, now cited: but I can see no justice in attempts to load me with unmerited censure, whilst that which was the most reprehensible measure of the embassy, is from partial motives passed in silence. nothing is said by Mr Pickering of General Pinckney's remaining in France after he was desired to depart, of his not leaving his sick daughter with his Wife, or his remaining long after I left it, on all which I shall make no comment.

9^{thly} Mr Pickering is entirely silent, in regard to the good effects of my stay at Paris, which terminated in an express renunciation on the part of France *first* of loans.—2dly of *reparations* for the Presidents speeches, whether considered as mulcts, or as douceurs. 3dly of an assumption by the United States, of debts due to their citizens from the Government, or citizens of France; 4^{thly} of a dissolution of the british treaty. 5^{thly} of exceptions to our claims not supported by a *role d'equipage*. [crew list] & also in advances on the part of France towards a new negotiation: measures opening wide the door to peace, & acceptable, I trust, to all who wish for it.

10^{thly} Events have proved my information to be good, "that the executive directory were very desirous of a reconciliation between the republicks," notwithstanding the labored representations of Mr Pickering to the contrary. the publication of the despatches naturally promoted the directory to vindictive measures; but these were renounced, & had they not been, means were wanting to gratify them. moreover the Directory was strongly urged, by its interest, to a reconciliation with this country. inasmuch as the enemies of France, who must have been highly gratified by a war between her, & the United States, could alone have profited by it, whilst her losses in consequence of it, must have been incalculable.

11^{thly} Mr Pickerings assertion "that professions" furnished the only ground on which Mr Gerry could form his opinion, that "before the arrival of the despatches of the Envoy's, the minister was sincere & anxious to obtain a reconciliation"—is without foundation. I regard not what a politician *says*, but what he *does*, his *conduct*, in my mind, is the *criterion* of his principles, & professions, & his *interest*, if it can be assertained, is an additional *test*. Mr Talleyrand was suspected, as I was well informed, by the directory, of commercial, territorial connections in the United States: & this opinion was confirmed in my mind by collateral information, which I obtained on, the subject. his professions, conduct, & interest, therefore all concurred to prove that he ardently wished for peace, from *private views*, if the public considerations I have mentioned can be supposed to have had no weight with him. his general system moreover was reputed & believed to be pacific with all the powers of Europe. These remarks, being not intended to influence any opinions, in regard to the french Government, or minister further than they have been blended by Mr Pickering with such as relate to my conduct, have only for their object, justice to myself. the experience which I had, by a long acquaintance with the President of the United States, of his love of justice, prompted me to accept a mission including as it did two other envoys, to an highminded, victorious, & irritated Government. the task I knew to be arduous, as it respected the embassy, & an ardent desire to satisfy my fellow citizens, then unhappily divided by violent parties; but I accepted it, in confidence that every allowance would be made in a negotiation, which promised merely a choice of difficulties; that my conduct would be fairly represented, & that, if in any respect it should appear exceptionable, I should be permitted to explain, before I was judged. the Presidents assurance since my return, that "he was well satisfied my conduct was upright, & well intended," has given me cordial satisfaction. God Almighty is a witness that in this he has judged rightly, & I flatter myself that however desirable at first blush it might have [sentence incomplete]

NOTES

1. Jean-Jacques Burlamaqui (1694-1748), Swiss philosopher; author of *Principes du droit de la nature et des gens*.

2. Emmerick de Vattel (1714-1767), Swiss philosopher and jurist of international law.

The recipient's copies of the following letters addressed to Thomas Jefferson are in the Jefferson Papers, Library of Congress. They are also reproduced in *Some Letters of Elbridge Gerry of Massachusetts* (Worthington Chauncey Ford, Brooklyn, New York, 1896).

TO MR. THOMAS JEFFERSON

Cambridge 15th January 1801

By Judge [Levi] Lincoln, my dear Sir, I embrace a favourable opportunity of acknowledging your very friendly letter of the 26th of Jany, 1799; but permit me previously to give you some information in regard to this gentleman. Mr Lincoln is an eminent lawyer in this state, & his professional talents, are accompanied with a humane & benevolent disposition, pure integrity, great liberality, & unsullied honor & morality; he is moreover a rational consistent & thorough republican. if you do not find that his character corresponds with this description, & that he is a real acquisition to Congress, I will readily relinquish all pretensions to any knowledge of mankind.

I congratulate you, my friend, very sincerely, that we have reason to hope never again "to see the day, when, breathing nothing but sentiments of love to our country, & its freedom & happiness, our correspondence must be as secret as if we were hatching its destruction." I have long wished to express the great obligation I felt, for your free & full communication by the letter mentioned; but to do it by the corrupt channel of a post office, or by any one, who betraying his trust, might consider perfidy as a meritorious act of federalism, was less eligible than to delay it till an interview or safe conveyance should present itself. as to my political sentiments, they are not secret, but I wish not to have them promulged by the base means of interception; because one seldom writes to a friend with that precision, which is necessary in expressing, during the reign of faction, political opinions. indeed, before the receipt of your letter I had every reason to suspect, that a certain disgraced & disgraceful ex-secretary [Timothy Pickering] opened a letter which I wrote to President Adams, & fabricated with its coadjutors, a report in regard to my communications which

[74]

the President was under the necessity of rejecting, as containing, "misrepresentations, calumnies, & falsehoods." But that tool & scapegoat of faction after having done more mischief than ever before was affected by a man of such mean & rude abilities, has retired to the woods, the proper situation for savage manners. could you conceive sir after seeing his report on my communications, that he was in possession of a proposition which I made to my colleagues, at the very commencement of our disgraceful conferences with X & Y, which would have put an end to them, & which President Adams acknowledged to me, was a full answer to everything that could be urged against me. it is in these words "To the question, whether the propositions informally & confidentially communicated to us as private citizens, at the request, as is stated of Mr Talleyrand, in his private capacity, will be adopted as the basis of a treaty? this answer is given, that it is highly probable some of the propositions communicated on the evenings of the 19th & 20 of October (being the 28th & 29th vendimaire) will be considered as the basis of the project of a treaty, & others as inadmissable; but that it is impossible to discuss, or come to a decision on them, until they are presented to us in our official characters." I have the original proposition by me, & at the bottom of it this note in General Pinckney's hand writing, "intended to be given Saturday the 21st of October." I have in a number of remarks, pointed out to the President, the illiberality, partiality & injustice of that officious report, & but for the President's request to avoid a public discussion of that extraordinary mission, would have, long ere this, done justice to my conduct & character. I trust however he will eventually do it.

I am extremely anxious to hear the result of the Presidential election. the insidious plan of the *federalists*, to place Mr [Aaron] Burr in the chair, is the acme of their perfidy and enmity to this country. he himself considers it in this light; well knowing, that the measure does not proceed from any respect or attachment to him, whom they abhor as well as yourself on account of your mutual predilection for republicanism, but from a desire to promote that division among the people, which they have excited & nourished as the germ of a civil war. I must candidly acknowledge, that I tho't it the best policy to re-elect Mr Adams & yourself; because in that event, you would have united your exertions & respective parties in suppressing the federalists, & at the next choice there was little reason in my mind to doubt, that Mr Adams would retire, &, with his friends support your election to the chair & administration: whereas there is danger now, that many of his adherents will again unite with the Hamiltonians & embarrass your administration, if you should succeed him, to avenge what they consider as an act of ingratitude to the object of their choice. but every friend to this country, in this event, will double his exertions to support you as a measure of the last importance to the foreign & domestic peace, & general welfare of the Union.

The silent & dignified contempt, with which you have treated the unparalleled abuse, which, to the eternal disgrace of the United States, has been circulated in their gazette, will be a distinguished trait in your character: I wish the venerable Doctor Priestly,[1] whose reputation, in the opinions of liberal men was invulnerable, had not condescended to notice anonymous calumnies. for the measure being unnecessary, was of no service to him. to confound slanderers, it is sufficient not to merit the slander.

Your assurance, in regard to your not having intermeddled with the affairs of our mission, by means of Doctor Logan,[2] was unnecessary: I knew you too well to listen to such a calumny. You have been pleased to make me "a profession of your political faith" & to add, "these my friend are my principles, they are unquestionably the principles of the great body of our fellow citizens, & I know that there is not one of them which is not yours also." in this last expression you do me great honor & justice likewise, & the principles are such as I ever have been, & hope in this country where I mean to spend the residue of my life, I ever shall be free to avow, & altho' "we differed on one ground, the funding system," yet was I sure that "from the moment of its being adopted by the constituted authorities, you became religiously principled in the sacred discharge of it, to the uttermost farthing." Your declaration to this effect therefore was not requisite to confirm my belief.

[76]

The corrupt propositions made by X & Y did not appear to me to have been sanctioned by the Directory of whose integrity or justice I had however no great opinion. indeed there was no positive evidence that they proceeded from Mr Talleyrand, but I have no doubt of the fact. £50,000 sterling, which as a douceur to be divided amongst the Directory, would at that time have been spurned at by them, might have answered the purposes of Mr Talleyrand & of the principal officers of his bureau, & his general character will warrant the belief, that this was his object: but be this as it may, you would never have seen those dispatches, had I been alone on the mission, untill all hopes of peace were at an end, & their communication had become necessary to unite the nation in a declaration of war. I was apprehensive of their publication & suggested to one at least of the other Envoys, General Marshal, the propriety of confining the communication to the President, & frequently to both, the extraordinary light if published, in which it must be viewed by men of sense. indeed it is wonderful that the promulgation of our dispatches had not proved fatal to me, for the Directory were so exasperated at it, as immediately to agitate the question of war, & there was a bare majority against it, on the principle only, that it would be a measure, which however provoked by the United States, was a favourite object of Great Britain & if adopted, would make France a dupe of the policy of that nation & of its own resentment. The great exertions of the british cabinet to circulate thro'out Europe our dispatches, served to convince the Directory of the impolicy of a war with us, at least on that occasion. Mr Talleyrand had early in the spring declared to me in the name of the Directory, that my departure from Paris would bring on an immediate rupture, & as there had been no instance of an official declaration made by the directory which had not been carried into effect, I have no doubt of it in this instance: but when they saw how eager their most inveterate enemy was to attain the object, they did not think so lightly of it, as they had been wont to consider it. the war party here have pretended, that the martial attitude of the U. States prevented a war, but that was not known in France at the time of the declaration made to me in the name of the directory, neither was a war viewed by it then, as an acquisition of such importance to G. B. if however there exists the least doubt that france would have declared war, or that a suggestion of X & Y to this effect, disavowed as it was by the directory and french minister, was different from the official declaration made to me by Mr Talleyrand, yet I think there can be no doubt, that had all the Envoys have left France at that critical period, the U. S. on their arrival here would have been so hurried away by passion & influenced by faction, as to have rendered the act very popular if not indispensable on the part of Congress.

Mr Pickering in his report has mentioned the threat of X & Y, as a measure proceeding from the directory, and comparing it with the declaration made to me says they both merited contempt, but the one was unofficial & has been disavowed, the other was official and by my correspondence, has been confirmed. judge then of his want of either discernment or candor, & whether it was not my indispensable duty to have remained in France, after the departure of the other envoys. you appeal to me to say whether peace might not have been attained, if either of my colleagues had been of the same sentiment with myself, I have no hesitation to answer in the affirmative, & to assure you candidly that your opinion that one of them at least possessed this qualification, was the point on which my determination, then held in suspense, turned for accepting the appointment to that embassy. without such a persuasion nothing could have induced me to the measure. but you was unfortunately for me, tho' perhaps fortunately for the publick, mistaken & the late events have proved, that peace as we both supposed, was attainable. Judge Lincoln has called on me rather sooner than I expected, & is in too much haste to wait untill I can answer the other parts of your letter: I must therefore reserve this for another opportunity.

I have thus far communicated without reserve & in the fullest confidence my sentiments on our important national concerns; & if they are too much tinged with severity, the unmerited provocation which I have had must be my apology. permit me now my dear sir to renew my assurances of the most sincere attachment, & that I remain with the highest respect your affectionate

friend

His Excellency
Mr Jefferson

E. Gerry

excuse errors for I cannot revise or correct this letter.

NOTES

1. Joseph Priestly (1733-1804), English scientist, clergyman, educator and writer on politics and theology.

2. George Logan (1753-1821), Physician, United States Senator, and friend of Thomas Jefferson. His unsanctioned negotiations induced the United States Congress to enact 30 January 1799, the so-called "Logan Act."

TO MR. THOMAS JEFFERSON

Cambridge 20th Jany 1801

My dear Sir

I now propose to finish my letter of the 15th, which was hastily concluded, to prevent inconvenience to my friend Lincoln.

In revising your political faith, I am not clear, that we perfectly agree in regard to a navy. I wish sincerely, with yourself, to avoid the evils pointed out, as the result of a powerful navy. the expense & extensive operation of an immense naval establishment, if our resources would admit of it, might make us more haughty & enterprising than wise, an object of the envy, jealousy & hatred of some or of all the maritime powers, & finally, the victim of our own "aristocracy": & every one is left to judge from his own observations, whether this is not the natural tendency of an overgrown navy. but at the same time it appears to me expedient, if not necessary, to extend our views to such a naval establishment as will furnish convoys to our valuable commerce, & place us, at least, above the depredations & insults of small maritime powers. with this qualification, I readily confirm the avowal of your political faith as my own.

Indulge me with some observations on the war party's adroitness, to take the credit to themselves of events, which they have labored abundantly to prevent, & to ascribe these, when popular, to means which they had adopted to promote a contrary effect. the martial attitude of the U. S., which is said to have prevented a war, & which I have before stated was not known in France at the time of the official declaration made to me, "that my departure from France would bring on an immediate rupture," did not then exist, as will appear by attending to facts. On the 18th of March, 1798, the French minister, in his letter to the Envoys of that date, signified the determination of the directory not to treat with two of them, & their readiness to open a negotiation with me. on the 23rd of March Mr Pickering enclosed to the envoys the President's instructions directing them, under certain circumstances, to put an end to the negotiation, & to demand their passports; & those instructions were delivered to me on the 12th of May. it must therefore be evident, that at the period of my resolution to remain in France, the martial attitude, so much boasted of, could not have been known there; because it did not then exist in the U. States. indeed if it had existed, it could not possibly have appalled France, in the zenith of her power; altho', as an evidence of her contempt, it might have prompted her to a declaration of War. but it is very curious, when the Congretional (*sic*) declaimers wish'd, to make the war party popular, they held up the martial attitude, as the chef d'oeuvre which prevented war; & when the principals wish'd to point the indignation of that party against the person whom they suppos'd to have merited it, they then asserted that he committed the unpardonable crime, & thus prevented the U. S. from rising to the highest pitch of national glory, by joining the coalition against France. this I am informed is stated in the late pamphlet issued from a prostituted press of that party at New York. peace with France was a measure of the last importance, in my mind, to the U. States; a war, wantonly provoked with her, would have made her vindictive & implacable, to the last degree, against this country; would have divided, & thus have weakened the nation; would have been immediately followed by a treaty, offensive & defensive, with G. Britain; would have made us completely dependent on her; would on her part have promoted an hauteur & insolence proportionate to that dependence; & would finally have left us the alternative only, of being reunited to her government or of being left by a separate treaty of peace between her & France, victims to the vengeance of that exasperated & powerful republick. it is evident then, that if in efforts for preventing war there has been any merit, the war party are so far from a claim to it, as to be justly chargeable with having made every exertion to promote that fatal event.

The delicate situation in which I was placed, by the rejection of the other envoys & by the declaration of the directory in regard to my departure, induced me to consider in every point of View, the effect of every measure which suggested itself; & that which was adopted, a proposition that the French government should come forward with the project of a treaty, & by the joint efforts of their minister & myself should acommodate it to the views & interests of the two nations; & that a French minister should be sent to our government to complete the business, will appear, I think, to have been the best, & would in a short time have been carried into effect, had not the Sophia arrived, or other measures intervened to defeat the proposition. but what, at that time, would have been the fate of the French minister & his project, even if the latter had contained provisions, exceeding the most sanguine expectations of the U. States? or in what manner would similar provisions, presented by myself to the government in any form of a treaty, been received, at a time when revenge for real or supposed injuries took place of a principle of accommodation, & when, with many, not to be mad, was to be a traitor? it was indeed fortunate, all circumstances considered, that measures were not so matured, as to have been presented in any form to our government, either by a French minister or by myself, as their rejection must have increased the irritation on both sides, & have rendered more difficult a reconciliation; & it was not less fortunate, that my communications had a tendency to, & with the operation of other causes really did, produce the effect you predicted.

That in the first place I was abused, in some measure by republicans, was to me evident; for I had seen at paris, in the American newspapers severe strictures on my first conference with Mr Talleyrand: but I agree with you, that they did not proceed far in their censures, & that the war party were malignant to excess. the "report" of Mr Pickering I saw, "his letters & conversation," I knew nothing of, or even the President's last instructions, until published; but the former produced such an indignation & ineffable contempt for the man, as determined me at once to expose his partiality, malignity, & injustice; & disagreeable as it always is to the publick, to see ministers of the same embassy contending with each other, I nevertheless determined to enter the lists with either or both of the other envoys, if they had come forward as Pickering's coadjutors. decency & propriety required, that after the request of the President, stated in my last, I should wait till his return, & till he could have an opportunity to explain matters. this he did without reserve, & communicated the breach, between himself & Pickering, produced in the first instance by the rejection of the most virulent parts of his report on my communications, & evidenced by the President's nomination of new Envoys to France. this information changed the complection of affairs, & as the plan of the war faction, of which Mr Pickering was prime agent, was to bring on me the whole of Mr Adams' as well as their own adherence, it was incumbent on me to defeat its purpose. I therefore communicated my remarks & strictures on Pickering's report to the President, & confided in him to do me justice. At that time the President had probably determined to dismiss Pickering, and whether he (the President) tho't that the disgrace of itself, altho' the result of intrigues against himself, was full satisfaction for the intrigues against me, or whether he tho't that a direct vindication of me would be trampling on a fallen foe, & perhaps implicate himself in some degree for having passed the report, no publick notice has been taken on the injustice sustained by me. indeed there was one consideration, in regard to a publick discussion of the affairs of the mission, which, independent of the disgrace generally attending public disputes & attaching itself to all parties, had great weight in my mind. immediately after the publication of my communications, & the nomination of new envoys, such a calm took place of the tempest which had before agitated the publick mind, as to promise a change of publick opinion; & the promise has been fulfilled to an extraordinary degree; in so much, as the war faction, who by means of the presses & their general arrangements, had in most of the states, & in this in particular the controul of the public opinion, at that time, are now generally execrated, if that happy state of tranquility, at the moment of it's return had been again interrupted by a discussion, which must inevitably have engaged the warmest passions of all parties, it was impossible to ascertain whether it could be again restored: & the greater the flame which might have been produced, the more would it have served the purposes of the war party: for their success depended on influencing the passions, & the republicans' success influencing the reason, of the people at large. but before a war should have been declared, & thereby our independence have been placed, as it inevitably must have been, on a precarious footing, I would have stated minutely every circumstance of the embassy, without regard to or consideration of delicacy, or of the feelings of any man. this I would have done, at the risk of personal destruction, for whilst the war party, faithfully rewarded the other envoys for declaring explicitly in favor of war, & "beamed" as you well express it, "meridian splendor" on them, not a solitary line was drawn in my favor: whilst "homage" was paid to a molten calf, whilst the continent was alive as the other envoys passed to their homes, the land ransacked for dainties to enrich the tables every where spread for them, & the imagination racked to invent toasts & publish eulogies in their praise, for having pursued measures, ruinous as we conceived, to their country: the most profound silence in every respect was observed by the real federalists & true republicans towards me, altho' at every hazard of my property life & reputation, & even of the welfare of my family, I had stood in the gap, on a forlorn hope, to repel a desperate enemy. indeed, a few days after my arrival, the french faction at Boston, signified, that they wished to take publick notice of me, & only waited for me to come out in the papers, as the other envoys had done, in favor of a War. My answer which undoubtedly exasperated them, was that I did not consider myself as the minister of any one State, Country (*sic*) or town, much less of a few individuals of the latter; that I was accountable to the Government only of the United States, that I had rendered to it a statement of my whole conduct, & the government may make what use it pleased of my communications; but that I should take no other measures, & wanted not any notice, as it was called, taken of me, on that or any occasion. indeed the ridiculous folly of the epicurean clubs and their toasts, reflected in my mind dishonor on the persons, who to attain such Eclat could submit to be managed & played off as political puppets: & to sell their birthrights, for a mess of pottage. that I was "secretly condemned to oblivion," by that party, that they wished to have had me "guillotined, sent to Cayenne," or the temple, to be sunk in the sea, or been sacrificed by a mob, that they stood ready to write me down, as they expressed it, to attack me by all the vile & vulgar means of ribaldry, carricatures & effigies I had no doubt; & on my arrival had certain information that the mine was charged & train layed: yet the apprehension of this, disagreeable as it must be to any one, did not deter me from discharging my duty to the public. but when the friends of the revolution & independence of this country appeared by their silence to be overawed on this occasion, how could they expect that I would "come forward", take, as you pleased to term it, "the high ground of my own character, disregard calumny" & depending on the meer presumption of being "borne above it, on the shoulders of my grateful countrymen", take a step, which in regard to its effect, was at least problematical, & if unsuccessful would have been condemned probably by the republicans as rash & impolitic, & most assuredly by the war party, as vindictive & inflammatory. this party long before my mission to France gave unequivocal proof that they wished to place & keep me in the background that "I was never to be honored or trusted by them, & that they waited to crush me forever, only, till they could do it without danger to themselves"; but this gave me no concern, I was above their favors, not being in quest of public office, or disposed to receive it at their hands, & above their frowns, viewing with indifference their impotent malice, whilst the country was free from the system of thralldom they were plotting against it. to prevent this I shall be ever ready to encounter any danger.

I recollect to have seen the expression you allude to of a member of Congress, unknown to me, that "to have acted such a part, I must have been a fool or madman." if his conduct on that occasion did not, in the public opinion, prove him to be both, it must have been for this reason only, that he was below public consideration & contempt. I have been prolix, I could not avoid it, because you desired me to be explicit. my mind revolted at the idea of burning your 2d & 3d leaves, but rather than have exposed my friend, I would, after answering your letter, have promptly complied with your wish. the danger being now passed, I shall defer it, untill I have the pleasure of again hearing from you.

I will now, my dear Sir, bid you adieu for the present, with an assurance of the highest respect & sincerest attachment, & that

I remain your affectionate friend

E. Gerry

His Excellency
Mr Jefferson.

EPILOGUE

"Alas, the last compatriot is gone. . . . A Friend who was neither warped nor shaken by change of time or fortune. . . . Faction may rave & party spirit slander, but an honester man he has not left behind nor a more sincere disinterested Friend of his Country."[1]

1. Quotation from a letter written by Abigail Adams 12 December 1814 informing her sister Mrs. Elizabeth Peabody of the sudden death of Elbridge Gerry. Gerry Collection, Russell W. Knight, Marblehead, Massachusetts.

Index

Davies, William R., 16
De jure belli atque pacis, 10
De jure naturae et gentium, 10
Deacy, Mrs. Sophie Chiluk, 6
Deblois, Mr., 41
Delft, 13
Della Moneta, 10
Demours (oculist), 41, 42, 43
Dialogues sur le commerce des blés, 10
Dickason, Mr., 26-28, 30-34, 36, 39-41
Dill, Captain H. Joseph, 26, 39
Directoire, French, 5, 9, 15-17, 19-21, 23, 30, 33, 36, 39, 46, 61, 67, 81
Dobree, P. F., 40, 41
Does, Sir Robert, 22
Dutch bankers, 8, 33
Dutch navy, 18

E

Elementa jurisprudentia univer-salis, 10
Ellsworth, Oliver, 16
England, 29, 30, 35, 39
Epilogue, 86

F

Farwell, Mr., 36
Fauxbourg, 24
Fiske, John, 24, 25
Flanders, 13
Florence, M., 34
Ford, Worthington C., 74
Foster, Bossenger, 8, 10, 14, 16-19, 24, 36
France, 16, 19, 31-33, 36-38, 42,
45, 46, 48, 50, 52, 55, 56, 66, 69, 77, 80-82
Franklin, Benjamin, 27
Freeman, Douglas S., 8
French Directoire, 5, 9, 15-17, 19-21, 23, 30, 33, 36, 39, 72, 80
French loan, 49-52, 55

G

Galiani, Ferdinand, 9, 10
Galvani, Luigi, 42
Gamage, Dr. William, 35
Gambol, Mr., 36
Geddis, Captain Henry, 41
George Washington (biography), 8
Germany, 29
Gerry, Ann, 29, 32, 35, 44
Gerry, Ann Thompson (Mrs. El-bridge), 7-9, 11, 15, 17, 20-22, 26, 28, 33, 36, 37, 40, 41, 43
Gerry, Catharine, 24-26, 28-30, 34, 35, 38, 42, 43
Gerry Collection, 37, 86
GERRY, ELBRIDGE: arrival at Bos-ton, 44; arrival in Europe, 7, 13; arrival in Paris, 11, 14; biog-raphy, 6, 10; birth of his fifth child, 22, 24, 25; books needed, 9, 10; calumnies and falsehoods, 75, 76, 84; censure, 5, 57, 82; condemnation, 5, 83, 84; con-ferences with Talleyrand, 44, 45, 47; death, 86; delay in de-parture from France, 37; depar-ture for America, 41, 44; dis-satisfaction of the French Direc-tory, 33; failure of the mission to Paris, 16, 20, 21, 23, 29, 33,

36; hopes of embarking for home, 41, 42; indignities, 5, 84; invitations from Talleyrand, 23, 30, 46, 57, 58; irritation of the French Directory, 67, 77; letters to John Adams, 44, 56, 60; letters to Thomas Jefferson, 74, 79; lodgings in Paris, 22; need of books, 9, 10; no prospect of success, 30, 31, 34; obloquy, 5; offer to leave France, 33, 34, 37; preparations for leaving Paris, 41, 54; secretaries, 10, 11, 36; sincerity, 86; sojourn in Paris, 5, 22; stigma, 58, 86; travels, 10, 11, 12, 14; unjust implications, 59, 61, 75; unmerited abuse, 5, 47, 60, 74, 78, 81

Gerry, Elbridge Junior, 27, 28, 32, 35

Gerry, Eliza, 29, 32, 35, 41, 43

Gerry, Helen Maria, 28, 31, 32, 35, 39, 42

Gerry, James T., 25

Gerry, John, 25

Gerry, Sarah, 25

Gerry, Thomas R., 27, 28, 32, 35

Ghent, 13

Giraud, Marc-Antoine A., 37, 38, 39

Grand-Jeans, Dr., 27, 31, 34, 43

Great Britain, 31, 48, 52, 55, 69, 77, 78, 80

Grotius, Hugo, 9, 10

Grove Street Cemetery, 25, 29

H

Hackett, Margaret, 6

Hague, The, 7, 10, 11, 13, 16, 17, 19

Halles, Les, 15

Harlem, 13

Harper, Robert G., 8

Havre, Le, 9, 22, 26, 30, 39, 44

Hebria (ship), 30, 39

Hellevoetsluys, 7, 13

Hingham, Mass., 37

Holland, 10, 14, 16, 69

Hood, Alexander, 15

Hope (ship), 20

I

Ireland, 35

Italy, 29, 69

J

Jackson, Captain, 26, 28

Jefferson Papers, 74

Jefferson, Thomas, 6, 44, 74, 79, 85

Jeffries, Dr. John, 27

Jenks, Captain Scott, 15

Johnstone, Mr., 59, 60

K

King, Mr., 34, 39

Knight, Russell W., 3, 6, 37, 44, 86

Knox, Julia, 31

Knox, Lydia, 31, 38

L

Lee, William, 30, 32, 33, 39
Leffingwell & Pierpont, 15
Library of Congress, 74
Life of Elbridge Gerry, 10, 25
Lille, 13, 16
Lincoln, Judge Levi, 74, 78, 79
Logan, George, 76, 79
London, 9, 14, 17, 22, 27, 28, 30, 31, 33, 34, 36, 39, 41
Louis XVI, 27
Lucy (ship), 26, 39

M

Marblehead, Mass., 6, 20, 32, 37, 86
Marshall, John, 5, 7, 8, 10, 11, 13, 16, 21, 22, 33, 34, 36, 37, 39, 44-49, 53, 54, 56-59, 77
Marshall Tureene Tavern, 7
Mary (brig), 15, 24, 30, 39
Massachusetts, 20, 25, 26, 37, 38, 86
McDonough, Thomas, 36, 37
Mendiant (ship), 41
Menin, 13
Minerva (ship), 22
Mitchell, Stewart, 38
Moerdijk, Holland, 11, 13
Morgue, Mr., 33, 39
Morison, Samuel Eliot, 15
Murray, William V., 16, 18
Murray, Mrs. William V., 19

N

Nantes, 13, 40
Napoleon Bonaparte, 16, 30
Netherlands, the, 16
New Hampshire, 38
New Haven, Conn., 25, 29
New Letters of Abigail Adams, 38
New York, 8, 14, 15, 22, 26, 30, 39
Newfoundland, 12
Nutting, Captain Ebenezer, 11, 15, 17, 18, 20, 24, 38

O

Oeler's Hotel, 8
Orchies, 13

P

Palfrey, Mary, 32
Palfrey, Susan, 32
Palfrey, William, 32
Paris, 5, 7, 9, 11, 14-17, 19-23, 25-27, 29-31, 33, 34, 36-38, 40, 41, 43, 44, 67, 69, 71
Passy, 27
Peabody, Mrs. Elizabeth, 86
Peabody Museum, 6
Perkins, Elisha, 42
Peronne, 13
Philadelphia, 8, 22, 26, 36
Pickering, Colonel, 39
Pickering, Timothy, 40, 56, 58-61, 63-69, 71-74, 78, 80, 82
Pierpont, Mr., 13, 15, 16, 18
Pinckney, Charles C., 5, 7, 8, 10, 16, 19, 21, 22, 26, 30, 34, 36-39, 45-47, 49, 53-56, 72, 75
Pinckney, Mrs. Charles C., 7, 8, 11
Plymouth, Mass., 35
poissardes in Paris, 14, 15, 16
Priestley, Joseph, 76, 79
Prince, Job, 37

Prince, Mr., 19, 26, 36, 37, 39
Princeton University Library, 6
Principes du droit de la nature, 73
Pufendorf, Baron Samuel von, 9, 10, 69

Q

Quasi-War with France, 20

R

Ramsgate, 12
Rhode Island, 38
Rice, Jr., Howard C., 6
Robespierre, 23
Ross, Captain Alexander, 19, 20
Rotterdam, 7-11, 13, 17, 20
Roye, 13
Rozier, Jean F. P. de, 25
Rutledge, Major, 14, 16, 46

S

Salem, Mass., 6, 25, 32
Schwartz: see Vanderyuer
Scilly Islands, 12, 15
Senlis, 13
Shipton, Fred W., 6
Sissons, Captain, 22, 39
Skipworth, Fulwar, 44, 59
Some Letters of Elbridge Gerry, 74
Sophia (U.S.N.), 41, 42, 44, 81
South Carolina, 8
Spain, 20, 69
Swediaur, F. X., 27
Switzerland, 15, 29, 69

T

Talleyrand-Périgord, Charles M. de, 14, 15, 23, 30, 37, 44-46,
48-50, 53-55, 57-60, 63, 65-68, 73, 75, 77, 78
Thompson, Helen, 14, 15, 24, 27-29, 32, 38, 39
Thompson, James, 24
Tissot, André-Simon, 12, 15
Torbay, England, 12
Townsend, David S., 29
Traill, Captain, 34, 41
Trumbull, Mr., 67

U

Union (ship), 7, 18, 20
United States Navy, 25, 37, 41
United States Senate, 61, 62

V

Valenciennes, 7, 13, 16
Vanderyuer, Villemont & Schwartz, 17, 21, 26, 33, 44
Vanstaphorst & Hubbard, 21, 26, 33, 44
Vattel, Emmerick de, 68, 73
Versailles, 23
Viets, Henry R., 6
Villemont: see Vanderyuer
Villette, Charles-Michel, 22
Villette, Marquise de, 22, 23, 24, 25, 54
Virginia, 27, 36
Voltaire, 22, 23

W

Ward, Captain Benjamin, 15, 24, 30, 39
Ware, Dr. James, 27, 28, 31, 32, 34
Warren, Dr., 33

Washington, George, 8, 32
Watham, Dr., 31, 34, 40, 41
Wenzel (oculist), 41, 42, 43
West Indies, 13
Willink & Co., John & William, 8,
  17, 21, 26, 33, 44

Worsely, Captain, 40

X

XYZ Affair, 5, 55, 57-63, 65, 67,
  71, 72, 75, 77, 78